BRICKWORK
PROJECTS
FOR PATIO & GARDEN

BRICKWORK PROJECTS
FOR PATIO & GARDEN

Designs, Instructions and 16 Easy-to-Build Projects

ALAN & GILL BRIDGEWATER

CREATIVE HOMEOWNER®

Designed and created for IMM Lifestyle Books by AG&G Books.
Copyright © 2004, 2017 "Specialist" AG&G Books

DESIGNER: Kate Lanphier
EDITOR: Jeremy Hauck
ILLUSTRATORS: Gill Bridgewater and Coral Mula
PROJECT DESIGN: Alan and Gill Bridgewater
PHOTOGRAGHY: AG&G Books and Ian Parsons
BRICKWORK: Alan Bridgewater

Shutterstock photos: Artazum (page 16), Baptist (page 39 bottom right), bogdanhoda (page 21), cobalt88 (cell phone: page 7), Ozgur Coskun (page 31), Dream2551 (page 39 top), eightstock (rubber gloves: page 7), Scott E. Feuer (page 17), Gavran333 (goggles: page 7), Vladimir Gjorgiev (page 24 top), John GK (page 55), Ispace (dust mask: page 7), jiangdi (page 100 bottom left), Kjpargeter (plate compactor: page 22), Jill Lang (page 11), Alexander Lobanov (cement mixer: page 23), Maxx-Studio (first-aid kit: page 7), Zima Nadezhda (page 49), Pagina (page 108), prapann (plywood: page 23), PriceM (boots: page 7), randy andy (pages 9, 51), Peter Turner Photography (page 13 bottom).

Printed in Singapore

Current Printing (last digit)
10 9 8 7 6 5 4 3 2 1

Brickwork Projects for Patio & Garden: Designs, Instructions and 16 Easy-to-Build Projects is published by Creative Homeowner under license with IMM Lifestyle Books.

ISBN 978-1-58011-793-7

Library of Congress Cataloging-in-Publication Data

Names: Bridgewater, Alan, author. | Bridgewater, Gill, author.
Title: Brickwork projects for patio & garden / Alan & Gill Bridgewater.
Description: Mount Joy, PA : Creative Homeowner, [2017] | Includes index.
Identifiers: LCCN 2017014567 | ISBN 9781580117937 (pbk.)
Subjects: LCSH: Patios--Design and construction. | Brickwork.
Classification: LCC TH4970 .B743 2017 | DDC 690/.893--dc23
LC record available at https://lccn.loc.gov/2017014567

Creative Homeowner®, *www.creativehomeowner.com*, is an imprint of New Design Originals Corporation and distributed exclusively in North America by Fox Chapel Publishing Company, Inc., 800-457-9112, 903 Square Street, Mount Joy, PA 17552, and in the United Kingdom by Grantham Book Service, Trent Road, Grantham, Lincolnshire, NG31 7XQ.

CONTENTS

PREFACE

When we saw our first house—an isolated Victorian farmhouse—we were confronted with numerous red brick outbuildings which were all, to some degree, tumbledown ruins. However, the bricks were crisp and hard-edged, and the lime mortar soft—so much so that we were able to scrape the bricks clean. We decided to salvage bricks from the outbuildings to renovate and extend the main house. We made contact with a retired master bricklayer in the village, who was prepared to give advice.

We spent the next ten years working on our home—Gill scraping the bricks, and our two toddler sons doing their part. Of course it was hard work, and we made lots of mistakes, but we were spurred on by the excitement of it all. We had the time of our lives building everything from walls and arches through to pillars, posts, raised beds, paths, sheds and even the top half of a well!

The ambition of this book is to share with you all the pleasures of working with brick to create garden features. With each project, we take you through the procedures of considering the design and working out how it might be modified to suit your individual needs. We tell you how to use the tools and materials, and explain the essential techniques. Illustrations and photographs show how best to achieve the step-by-step procedures; in fact, we take you through all the stages of designing, making, constructing and finishing.

Brickwork doesn't require complex tools or specialized knowledge: it is about working with your hands in the garden, and the pleasure of using your mind and body to create exciting structures.

Best of luck!

Alan & Gill

The imperial measurements used in this book were converted from metric. However, in all cases, the original metric measurements are given in parentheses. For best accuracy, keep to one system and avoid using a combination of metric and imperial measurements.

HEALTH AND SAFETY

Gloves **Goggles** **Dust mask** **Earmuffs** **First-aid kit**

Cell phone **Rubber gloves** **Boots** **In-line GFCI**

- A few projects are physically demanding and if you have doubts about whether you are up to it, get advice from your doctor. When lifting heavy items, minimize back strain by holding the item close to your body, and bend your knees rather than your back.
- Never operate a machine, or attempt a difficult lifting or maneuvering task, if you are feeling tired.
- Follow manufacturers' instructions when using tools and materials.
- Keep a first-aid kit and phone nearby, in case of an emergency and, if possible, avoid working alone.
- Do not build a pond if you have young children. Other water features are safer, but even so, never leave children unsupervised.
- Use an in-line GFCI (between the power socket and the plug) when operating electrical tools and water pumps, to prevent electric shock.

- Brickwork—digging holes, breaking up hardcore and handling bricks—is tough on your hands, so wear hefty leather gloves whenever possible. You will probably have to take them off for minute tasks.
- When mixing concrete and mortar, wear waterproof, thick rubber gloves, which will protect your skin from contact with corrosive cement powder.
- Boots made from thick leather, preferably steel-toe boots, will protect your feet.
- Sometimes it is necessary to wear additional protective gear, especially when you are cutting materials that generate sharp chippings and a lot of dust. Wear goggles when you are smashing hardcore, cutting or breaking bricks, stone and concrete, and a dust mask when mixing cement powder.
- When using an angle grinder, wear heavy boots, gloves, goggles, a dust mask and earmuffs.
- Wear earmuffs when using any noisy machine.

BRICKWORK INSPIRATION

Bricks are wonderfully easy to handle and make building a pleasure. Any patio or garden structure made out of brick looks solid and imposing, and with their ability to fit into a wide variety of patterns and designs, nothing beats bricks for versatility in creative structure design. What's more, bricks seem to blend into their surroundings.

Rugged, natural and soft-textured, bricks possess an inherent beauty. Moreover, they come in a wide spectrum of colors, from slate blue and black to red and even creamy white, encompassing a rainbow of oranges, yellows and umbers along the way. When you add your own patterns, you can make any structure endlessly interesting to look at.

Three easy-to-follow approaches will allow you to enhance the visual interest of most brickwork projects: setting bricks in different patterns and formations, incorporating bricks of different colors, and harmonizing bricks with wood, stone or tile.

Traditional bond patterns like herringbone, basket weave and diaper formations offer ways to easily create exciting visual texture (see pages 48–49). To extend their design flexibility even further, bricks can be set with the frog face or the bottom face upwards, on their end (header), or on their side (stretcher—see page 27.) They can also be cut or angled.

Aside from patterning and using bricks of varying colors, a third way to add visual interest to brickwork is to develop the natural harmonies that bricks share with other natural materials, notably stone, tile and wood. The thoughtful incorporation of these other materials will complement the sturdy earthiness of bricks.

LEFT This urban haven echoes the brickwork of the surrounding edifices. The two-by-two basketweave pattern forms a sturdy and attractive patio, while the flower border edging cleanly separates the patio and the flower border.

ABOVE Everything about this rustic but formal staircase is in harmony, from the symmetry created by the arrangement of flowerpots to the interesting contrast between the worn red bricks and the green lines of moss just beginning to overtake the bricks. These wide steps, formed by bricks bedded on their stretcher sides in a running bond, rise gracefully to the entrance of a stately home. The wide landing could double as a patio.

BELOW A huge brick patio that encircles a low dwarf hedge (not shown) and looks rather like a very wide path. The patio is built to accommodate a sloping site—the outer edge is raised and the inner edge is flush with the turf by the hedge.

RIGHT This solidly well-built flight of steps connects a path to a beautiful brick courtyard. The design appears effortless, but in fact great care has gone into planning the overall brickwork scheme and incorporating steps that are subtly curved.

ABOVE A number of brickwork projects—path, columns, walls and flower border edging—comes together in an imposing "tied-in" structure. The path draws you through the gateway and turns to follow the wall; softening the picture, formal flowerbeds edged with bricks laid on their header faces divide path and wall.

The foundation under these weighty structures must be extensive, but the bricks protruding at the corners of the columns add a delicate touch, as do the blossoms peeping through the gaps in the honeycomb bond.

LEFT A traditional English Sussex farmyard wall with the bricks set in a heading bond (the courses run at a diagonal angle to the ground).

ABOVE A decorative, low-rise set of two steps in a country garden. Notice how the shape and sweeping arrangement of the steps leads the eye across the patio to the other steps and the lawn beyond. The framed herringbone pattern and recessed detailing must have been a challenge to build.

RIGHT The contrast between the even, square shapes of the brickwork and the curvy and rounded shapes of the landscaping adds visual interest to this cozy planted patio. Further heightening the complexity of the design is the variety of plants and the intersecting brickwork patterns. The rustic wood bench and the bright wall lend a softening, harmonizing touch.

LEFT The perfect circular shape of this raised garden pond, which must have required many bricks to build, would have been challenging to achieve, but it creates an ideal centerpiece to this formal garden. The aged look of the bricks makes for an appealing invitation to reflect on the scenic beauty. Note how the header splays used to form the rim of the pond create a seating area.

PART I: TECHNIQUES

DESIGN AND PLANNING

The art of working with bricks relies on the coordination between mind, hand and eye: the key words are planning, rhythm, repetition and timing. The trick is to fit the components together with the minimum of measuring and as few cuts as possible. If you do have to make a cut, the challenge is to get it right the first time! If you can use the bricks as you find them—new, salvaged, seconds or left over from another job—so much the better.

FIRST CONSIDERATIONS

- What do you want to achieve? Write down the aspects that are important to you, and look at magazines, books and other people's gardens to assess the possibilities. If necessary, change our project designs to suit your needs.
- Bricks are made in many colors and textures. Do some research into what is available, and see what you like.
- To make a project fit better into your space, you may have to consider changing its size, shape and proportions. Would it, for example, look better as a larger but low, long and thin structure, or as a square rather than round structure? Use the dimensions of a brick to dictate the precise overall project dimensions—working in a number of whole bricks wherever possible. (See pages 40–41 for how to cut bricks.)
- Location and orientation are important. Mark the envisaged position with sticks, plastic sheet or plywood, and look out for possible problems such as the blocking of routes through the garden, unfortunate viewpoints and the casting of shadows.
- If the project is a pond or water feature, does it require a long trench to be dug in the garden to bury a power cable, and is this possible?
- Are there parts of a project's construction that you don't understand? Try working out the problem on paper or mocking up the structure with real materials.
- Calculate the costs and time involved, to make sure that the project is feasible.

Choosing a suitable project

Sometimes it is easy to get carried away and build something massive that dominates the space and frankly looks out of place, because the scale is wrong and the style is not suitable. So before you decide what to build, take stock of your garden or yard and consider how to improve it. If it is cluttered, you may want to rebuild an existing feature to make it smaller, stronger or more decorative. If the area is a bombsite or a blank canvas, design the whole garden first; when you are ready to build brickwork projects, make sure they fit into the overall scheme.

Garden features are more than basic structures that are constructed out of necessity—they are also decorative. You may need to change the appearance or style of a project to suit your garden. For example, a simple, well-proportioned brick planter would suit a modern scheme, but for a Victorian garden, it would be more appropriate to incorporate detailing and decoration. From a safety point of view, avoid building ponds and some water features if you have young children.

Siting: Deciding where on the site—in the garden or on the plot—the structure is going to be placed. The aspect, sun, shade and proximity to the house may need to be taken into consideration.

Planning the project

The first part of a project (and one of the most important) is deciding on its precise size and location. For a patio outside your back door, for example, you need to know its finished height, how it slopes in order to drain rainwater away from the house, and its exact size to the nearest brick and mortar joint.

In the projects in this book, a lot of the planning has been done for you, but do take note of any advice or exceptions that suggest you might need to revise the design, and which refer you to a page within this techniques section. Do a survey of the site and draw simple scaled diagrams on graph paper, showing how the foundation is constructed and how the project is built. Some structures pose more obvious planning problems: steps, for example, have to conform to certain dimensions, otherwise you will trip over them; walls that are too high or long can lean or fall down without the benefit of extra support (see page 50).

Every brickwork project requires a foundation: a firm, level (or sometimes slightly sloping, in the case of a patio) base on which to build, otherwise it will collapse. It is very important to use an appropriate foundation, and to plan it

Trial run or dry run: Setting out the components of a structure, without using concrete or mortar, in order to ascertain whether or not the pattern of bricks is going to work out.

Planning: The procedure of considering a project, viewing the site, making drawings, working out quantities and costs, prior to starting work. Thorough planning is vital in order to avoid hold-ups and the wastage of materials.

in a drawing to show its size and depth. For example, if you want a patio to be level with the surrounding ground, the patio needs to take into account the thickness of the bricks that will be used for paving.

Buying the right tools and materials

Once you have figured out the project design in detail, you can assess what you need to build it. Sometimes, it is necessary to compromise with both tools and materials in order to make a project affordable. If that is the case, ensure you have enough time to do the work with basic manual tools, and don't resort to inferior materials that will deteriorate quickly.

If you don't have a wonderful set of tools, consider borrowing or renting better ones. A cement mixer is worth renting if you are working on a large project, unless you enjoy bodybuilding exercise! Call around for quotes for materials, and order in bulk when possible. The choice of bricks available depends on your location; you can also consider using second-quality bricks (rejects) or reclaimed (secondhand) bricks.

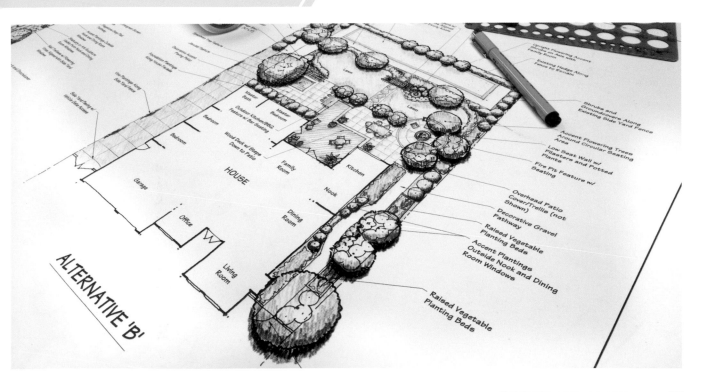

BRICKWORK DESIGNS FOR THE GARDEN

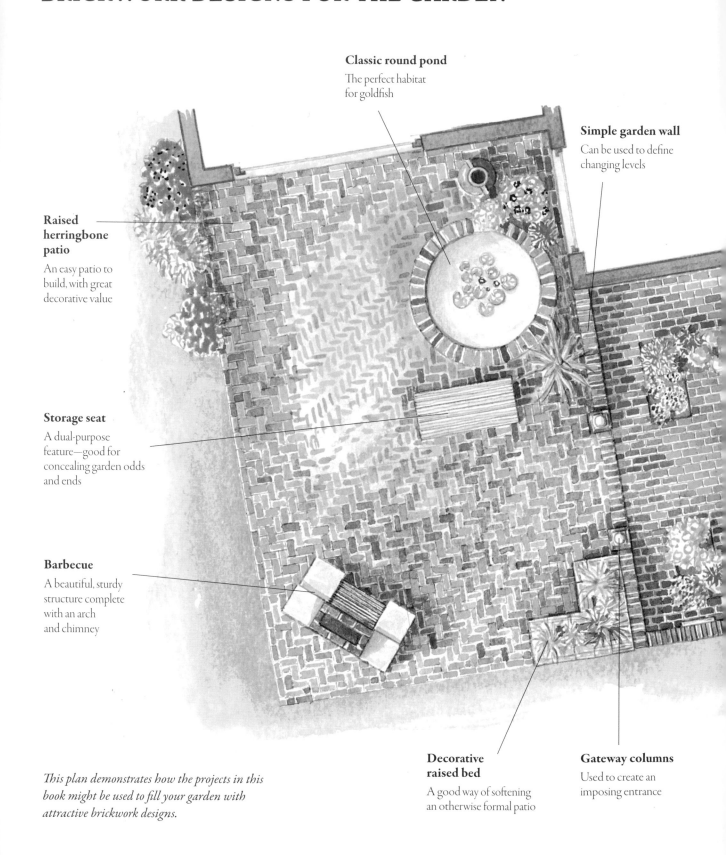

Classic round pond
The perfect habitat for goldfish

Simple garden wall
Can be used to define changing levels

Raised herringbone patio
An easy patio to build, with great decorative value

Storage seat
A dual-purpose feature—good for concealing garden odds and ends

Barbecue
A beautiful, sturdy structure complete with an arch and chimney

Decorative raised bed
A good way of softening an otherwise formal patio

Gateway columns
Used to create an imposing entrance

This plan demonstrates how the projects in this book might be used to fill your garden with attractive brickwork designs.

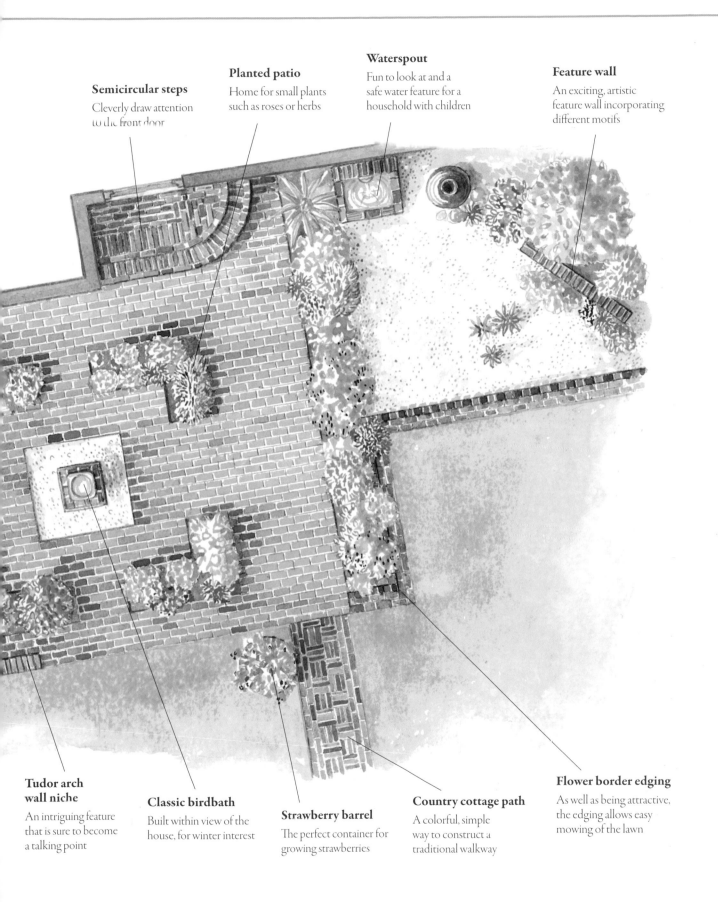

Semicircular steps
Cleverly draw attention to the front door

Planted patio
Home for small plants such as roses or herbs

Waterspout
Fun to look at and a safe water feature for a household with children

Feature wall
An exciting, artistic feature wall incorporating different motifs

Tudor arch wall niche
An intriguing feature that is sure to become a talking point

Classic birdbath
Built within view of the house, for winter interest

Strawberry barrel
The perfect container for growing strawberries

Country cottage path
A colorful, simple way to construct a traditional walkway

Flower border edging
As well as being attractive, the edging allows easy mowing of the lawn

TOOLS

You don't need many tools for brickwork, but they should be the best tools that you can afford. If you are working on a fixed budget, purchase top-quality trowels (a bricklayer's trowel and a pointing trowel) and a level (a traditional wood-cased one is best), and then save money by buying cheap shovels and so forth. The following pages describe essential items for the toolbox, and tools you may want to rent to make a job easier.

TOOLS FOR MEASURING AND MARKING

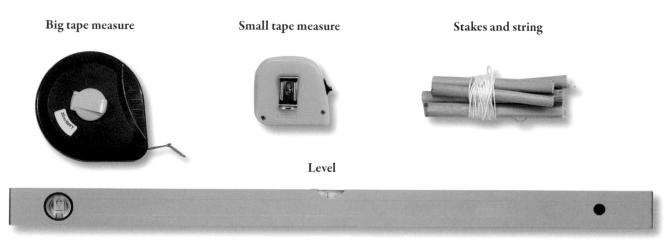

Big tape measure   **Small tape measure**   **Stakes and string**

Level

Measuring and marking out a site

If you are unfamiliar with garden projects and brickwork, it can be difficult to know how to begin. Everything starts from a foundation, so either build on an existing foundation such as a patio (see page 35), or dig out some earth and make a new foundation.

When building a foundation, use a tape measure (available in various lengths) to establish the dimensions, then mark the site with stakes and string (see page 34). If the shape is irregular, use marking chalk or spray paint. Dig out the foundation hole: the sides of the hole contain the foundation. Alternatively, wooden boards (formwork) can be used to construct an accurate frame to retain the foundation. A level is used when digging to a level depth. Waste should be removed from the site.

Measuring and marking during construction

The exact dimensions of brickwork projects are (or should be) governed by the proportions of a brick (see page 27), so you can either calculate the length and width of the first course, and mark it out on the new or existing foundation using a tape measure, straightedge and a piece of chalk; or arrange the bricks without mortar, judging the gaps between each brick, then nudge the layout straight and square and mark around it with chalk.

Once you have laid the first course of bricks, use a level to indicate the horizontal and vertical positions, and a straightedge to check for straightness. A line set (a line stretched between two stakes) is useful for guiding the courses of stone, and estimating course heights, on long lengths of wall (see page 91).

Leveling: Using a level to decide whether or not a structure or brick is level (horizontally parallel to the ground, or vertically at right angles to the ground), and then making adjustments to bring individual bricks into line.

TOOLS FOR MAKING FOUNDATIONS

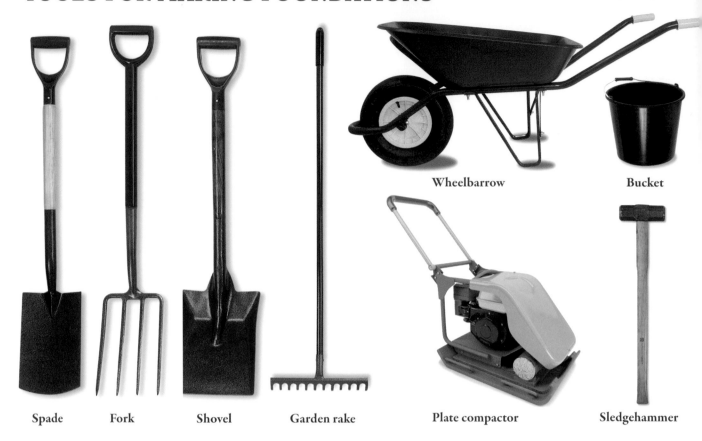

Spade   Fork   Shovel   Garden rake   Plate compactor   Sledgehammer

Wheelbarrow   Bucket

Removing turf and digging earth

Once the area of ground has been marked with string, chalk or paint, start digging and removing earth to create a clean-sided hole of a specific depth. A spade is used to slice through the turf, and a fork is very handy for removing the turf in square chunks. A wheelbarrow is essential for moving earth away from the site, and a bucket is useful for removing small quantities and when working in confined areas. The wheelbarrow and bucket are also employed for moving all other materials. To dig a hole in extremely hard or stony ground, specialty digging tools such as a pickaxe or mattock may be required.

Compacting hardcore

Hardcore (scrap brick, stone and concrete) must be compacted in order to form a firm base. A sledgehammer is used to break it up into smaller pieces and to beat these into the ground to make a compact, even layer. This can be notoriously hard work when dealing with large areas (over 20 square feet, or 2 square meters), so either get help or buy broken-brick hardcore, which is easier to break and consolidate. Always wear goggles to protect your eyes from chippings.

Spreading gravel, sand and concrete

Use a shovel for spreading gravel, sand, ballast (a mixture of gravel and sand) and concrete. A rake is useful for spreading dry materials evenly over a large area. A screed board is brought in to scrape off excess material to make a smooth and level surface to a specific depth, and is used for concrete, sand and ballast. It consists of a length of wood supported at either end by a frame (see page 65). Some patio foundations consist of dry materials, laid down without cement, and it is best to rent a compacting machine called a plate compacter to compress gravel, sand or ballast into a firm base (also for firming patio bricks into position).

Hardcore: Scrap bricks, stone and concrete crushed with a sledgehammer and leveled to provide drainage and support beneath a foundation. Alternatively, drainage rock, gravel or graded base can be used.

TOOLS FOR MIXING CONCRETE AND MORTAR

Shovel

Bucket

Plywood

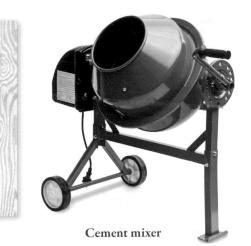

Cement mixer

Mixing by hand

Mixing concrete or mortar by hand is hard work. Find a sheet of exterior plywood for mixing on, about 4' (1.22m) square and ½"–1" (13–25mm) thick, a shovel and a bucket for the water (see page 37). If more than 55 lbs. (25kg) of cement or mortar is required, you should seriously consider using a cement mixer.

Using a cement mixer

A cement mixer is used for making concrete and mortar, and is a wonderful timesaver that actually does a better job than you can do by hand. Cement mixers can be bought or rented, and are available in different capacities, powered by an electric or gas engine. The small, electric versions are most suitable for DIY projects and mix up to approximately twelve shovelfuls of cement, sand or ballast, producing one wheelbarrow load of concrete or mortar. Follow the instructions supplied with the machine. Remember that at the end of a job, an empty cement mixer can only be left for about five minutes before it needs to be washed out, otherwise the remnants of cement will set solid. Use a hose and a brush to do this.

TOOLS FOR HANDLING MORTAR

Bricklayer's trowel

Pointing trowel

Spreading mortar

The bricklayer's trowel (the larger of the two similarly shaped trowels) is the one used most frequently in bricklaying. It is used to scoop up mortar and spread it smoothly, to an even thickness, over the top and ends of the bricks, and also for slicing off excess mortar that has squeezed out from between the bricks. It can also be employed to knock the bricks level (using the blade or the handle) or to chop bricks roughly in half.

Finishing joints

After the bricks have been laid and before the mortar is dry, the joints between the bricks need to be cleaned up with a pointing trowel or by another method (see page 47). The pointing trowel is used to fill any gaps in the joints, and also to repoint (see page 55). Be careful not to smear the excess mortar on the face of the brickwork. The pointing trowel may be used in place of the bricklayer's trowel if you find that too heavy and awkward.

TOOLS FOR CUTTING BRICK, STONE AND CONCRETE

CAUTION

Angle grinders and other hand-held disc cutters are dangerous machines and should only be operated while wearing protective gear (see page 43). Follow the manufacturer's advice, and if you have never operated one before, it's advisable to ask an expert or the tool rental store to show you how to use it safely.

Cutting bricks

To cut just a few bricks, for the projects in this book, we recommend using hand tools for the sake of simplicity. The most common method is to simply chop the bricks with a brick chisel and club hammer (see page 41).

Various machines are available for cutting brick and masonry (see page 41). You can use an angle grinder, brick guillotine (good for quick 90° cuts, but the results aren't as good as with a masonry saw), circular saw fitted with an abrasive masonry blade, or a disc cutter fitted with a stone-cutting disc. If your design requires hundreds of bricks to be cut, consider renting a masonry saw with a diamond blade (which will also cope with angled cuts).

Cutting blocks, slabs, stone and tiles

Concrete block pavers can be cut in the same way as bricks, as described above. Concrete slab pavers, flat pieces of stone and thick concrete or clay tiles can all be cut with a heavyweight disc cutter or masonry saw (depending on size). However, for safety reasons we recommend using a small angle grinder fitted with a stone-cutting disc to score a cut, and then finishing the cut with a brick chisel and club hammer (see page 42). Most thin tiles can be cut with a basic hand-operated tile-cutting machine.

Wear gloves and goggles when cutting by hand; if using a machine, wear gloves, goggles, a dust mask, earmuffs and sturdy boots.

Club hammer   **Bricklayer's hammer**

Angle grinder

Brick chisel

ADDITIONAL TOOLS

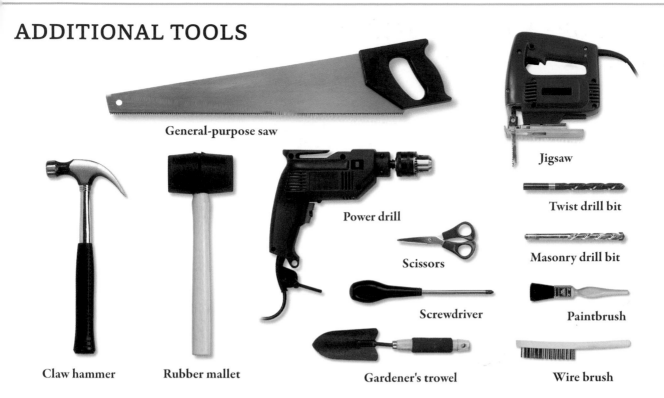

General-purpose saw

Jigsaw

Twist drill bit

Power drill

Masonry drill bit

Scissors

Screwdriver

Paintbrush

Claw hammer

Rubber mallet

Gardener's trowel

Wire brush

Woodwork

Sometimes the projects require you to use formwork (wooden frames) during the casting of foundations. Formwork usually consists of planks of wood laid square and level, held in place by stakes and nails (see page 29). A general-purpose saw (or crosscut saw) and a claw hammer are all that is needed to make it.

Simple brickwork arches are easy to build as long as you use a wooden former to establish the shape of the arch and support the bricks during the building process (see pages 124–129, 136–143, 144–151, 152–157). The former is made from plywood cut with an electric jigsaw, which is a safe and easy-to-use tool. After drawing the curved shape on the plywood (you may use a trammel for this—see page 46), hold down the plywood on the workbench, start up the saw (don't allow the blade to touch the wood until the motor is running) and gently guide the blade around the curve. Wear goggles and follow the manufacturer's instructions.

Drilling holes

A general-purpose power drill with hammer action is ideal for drilling jobs. For drilling wood, use twist bits for small-diameter holes (under ⅜" (10mm) in diameter), and flat or spade bits for larger holes. For drilling into brickwork and masonry, use masonry bits and set the drill to hammer mode. Always follow the instructions supplied with the tool.

Finishing

Once you have completed a project (or at the end of each day if you are conscientious), you will need to clear up the site and clean any blobs, splashes and smears of mortar off the brickwork and ground. Use a wire brush to scrub bricks (wear gloves and goggles). If you choose to apply a treatment to the surface of the brickwork in order to clean it (see page 54), use a paintbrush. A paintbrush is also used for any painting tasks such as sealing render with waterproofing paint, as in the water feature on page 157.

Miscellaneous

A rubber mallet is useful for bedding brickwork or masonry in mortar. It is soft, but heavy, and does the job without damaging the surface of the material. The wooden or plastic-covered handle of a club hammer or bricklayer's hammer will do a similar job. Other useful tools include a screwdriver for driving in screws (if you prefer them to nails) and a gardener's trowel for projects such as the Decorative Raised Bed and the Strawberry Barrel, where planting is required.

When building water features that employ lining materials, such as the Classic Round Pond, use scissors to cut the lining materials; use a hacksaw (a metal saw) to cut the armored plastic pipe used to protect electric cable and water pipe, in projects such as the Waterspout. Don't buy new tools until the need arises.

MATERIALS

For backyard garden projects, it is best to use well-fired (or high-fired) exterior-grade bricks, or engineering bricks, both of which are harder than ordinary bricks, with good frost resistance. Your first search, therefore, will be for a supplier who can provide good-quality bricks at low cost. You can cut costs dramatically by renting a flatbed truck and going to the supplier yourself. If you are lucky, there will be misshapes available at half the normal price—these bruised and battered bricks are perfect for garden projects. Avoid bricks that show cracks across their width.

BRICKS

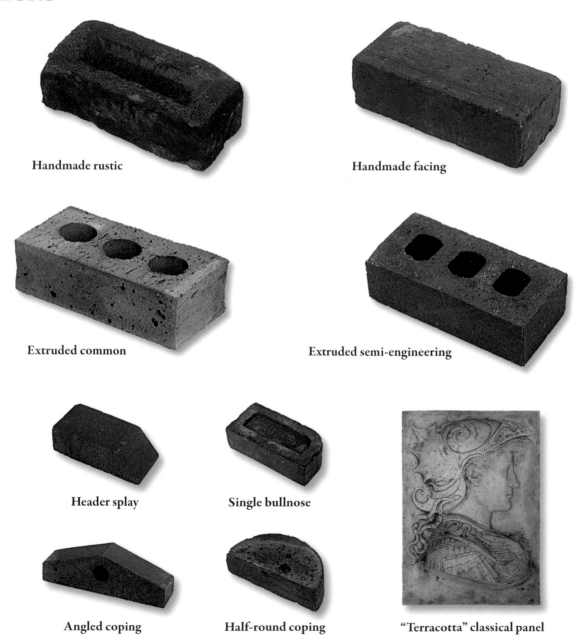

Handmade rustic

Handmade facing

Extruded common

Extruded semi-engineering

Header splay

Single bullnose

Angled coping

Half-round coping

"Terracotta" classical panel

Appearance

For most people, the most important aspect of brickwork is its appearance. Generally speaking, bricks are more attractive than other manufactured walling materials such as concrete or reconstituted stone. Use discretion when choosing bricks: some combinations of color and texture in modern bricks are ugly.

Study examples of finished brickwork to identify the types you like most. Remember, the characteristics of a brick are intensified when many bricks are placed together in a wall or patio. Bricks vary from area to area, because they are made from clay dug from the ground, and this varies in color and properties. They are also manufactured in different ways: machine-made bricks are the most accurately formed and easy to build with; handmade bricks look better but are a bit wobbly and more difficult to lay. The design and availability of special bricks varies according to region.

Properties

Bricks are manufactured for different purposes. "Facing" bricks are sold for their appearance. "Engineering" bricks are intended for situations where high strength and low water absorption are very important, and are not sold for their appearance. This type of brick is the most expensive, and you would probably only choose it for a particular situation, such as when building steps, because its extra strength and hardness guarantee that the edges of the steps will not crumble.

All bricks have a frost-resistance rating, varying from frost resistant, to moderately frost resistant, and not frost resistant (may only be used internally). We have used moderately frost-resistant facing bricks for the projects.

Bricks have six sides: two end or "header" faces, two side or "stretcher" faces, a top or "frog" face, and a bottom face. Most bricks have some kind of cavity to trap mortar—the frog is a rectangular recess in the top for this purpose (some bricks have three holes running right through the brick instead). Bricks with frogs are more versatile, as they have one flat surface that allows them to be used upside down as coping or paving.

Sizes

The dimensions of a brick are significant, and when you start building, you will soon realize why. They are a convenient size to handle, roughly twice as long as they are wide, and their height is roughly one third of their length. This means that they fit together perfectly in many kinds of construction. The precise sizes can vary according to the

Sourcing: Questioning suppliers by phone, email or letter, in order to make decisions concerning the best source for materials—especially sand, cement and bricks.

manufacturer and different sizes are common in different countries. Standard American and metric bricks may vary, and some bricks are made to match the size of old bricks.

Standard American bricks are 8" (20.3cm) long, 3⅝" (92mm) wide and 2¼" (57mm) thick. Allowing for ¼" (6mm) mortar joints, this gives a unit measurement of 8¼" (21cm), 3⅞" (98mm) wide and 2½" (64mm).

Metric bricks are normally 8½" (21.5cm) long, 4" (10.25cm) wide and 2½" (65mm) thick. When calculating the number of bricks required for brickwork, ⅜" (10mm) mortar joints are allowed for, giving a unit measurement of 8⅞" (22.5cm) long, 4⁷⁄₁₆" (11.25cm) wide and 3" (75mm) thick.

All the projects can be built using metric or standard bricks, although if standard bricks are used, the overall finished dimensions will be different to those specified. (See page 20 for how to mark out projects).

Other kinds of brick

If you want to use old bricks from a salvage yard, because you like their antique appearance, or want to match existing brickwork, be prepared to pay more than for new bricks. Avoid bricks with mortar still stuck to them, because it is tough work to chisel off.

"Seconds" (second quality) are bricks that are less than perfect— usually chipped, warped, cracked or damaged by under- or over-firing. Avoid cracked or under-fired bricks.

Many special brick shapes are available for specific and decorative purposes—see what's on sale and consider incorporating these into your projects to give added interest.

BUYING TIPS

- Never buy bricks without inspecting the product.
- When buying seconds, ideally it is best to select each brick individually.
- If you are renting a truck to collect the bricks yourself, it is much better to make several journeys with small loads, rather than a single journey with an overloaded vehicle.
- If you are having bricks delivered, plan in advance where they are to be unloaded, and make sure that they are not going to pose a hazard or obstruction.

FOUNDATION MATERIALS, MORTAR AND RENDER

Ballast   Gravel   Coarse sand

Builder's sand   Cement

Concrete, aggregates and ballast

Most foundations begin with hardcore—waste brick, stone and concrete, which is broken into pieces and compacted to provide a firm, interlocked base that allows water drainage. Normally, the foundation is completed with a layer of concrete.

Concrete consists of portland cement powder, fine aggregate (sand), coarse aggregate (gravel or crushed stone), and water. The shape and size of the particles of sand and stone in the aggregate decide the character of the concrete— its strength, hardness, durability and porosity. Ready-mixed aggregate can be bought in most home improvement stores. This mix of aggregates (coarse sand and small stones or gravel) is often called ballast. For the projects, pick an average mix made up of small-sized gravel and sand.

Some foundations for patios and paths omit the concrete—alternative foundations are: hardcore, gravel and sand; hardcore and ballast; or hardcore, ballast and sand. In each case, the hardcore, ballast and sand are compacted.

Sand

Sand is available in various types. Coarse sand is often used for making concrete, laying under paving, or is mixed with cement to make mortar for rendering. Builder's sand (also known as soft sand) is a medium sand used for making mortar. It can also be used for concrete and foundations (it is not as effective as coarse sand, but you may want to order one type of sand in bulk to do the whole job). Fine sand (also known as silver sand or kiln-dried sand) is ideal for filling the joints in brick and block paving (but use ordinary sand for large gaps).

Mortar

Mortar is a mixture of builder's sand, cement powder and water, and is used to stick bricks together. The ratio of ingredients is important and mixing takes practice (see pages 36–39). A mortar made with coarse sand produces a coarser mortar suitable for rendering. Render is a thin coating of mortar stuck to the surface of bricks.

WOOD AND PLYWOOD

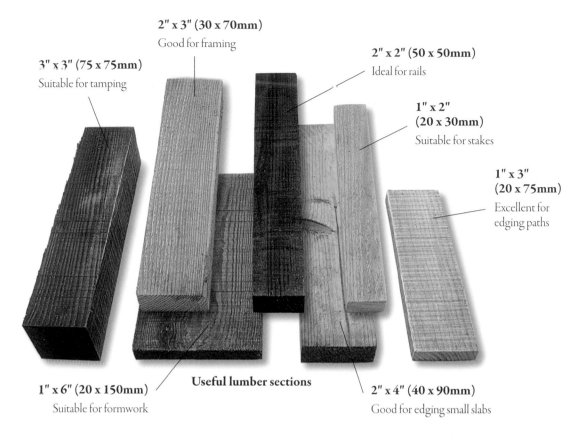

3" x 3" (75 x 75mm)
Suitable for tamping

2" x 3" (30 x 70mm)
Good for framing

2" x 2" (50 x 50mm)
Ideal for rails

1" x 2" (20 x 30mm)
Suitable for stakes

1" x 3" (20 x 75mm)
Excellent for edging paths

1" x 6" (20 x 150mm)
Suitable for formwork

Useful lumber sections

2" x 4" (40 x 90mm)
Good for edging small slabs

Plywood

Railroad tie

Formwork
Formwork is the wooden framing used to make a foundation. Use cheap, ready-sawn or reclaimed wood, as it will be ruined by the cement and usually serves no purpose after the foundation is complete. Plywood consists of thin layers of wood stuck together, and is ideal for making formers, which are the arched frames used to support brickwork arches during construction. It comes in standard-size sheets of 4' x 8' (1.22 x 2.44m), or smaller pieces cut from it.

Other uses
Wood goes well with brick—the warm colors look good together. Treated pine, oak or railroad ties can be incorporated into your garden projects.

During the construction process, cheap exterior-grade plywood (often called "shuttering" plywood) can be used to protect the area surrounding a project, guarding lawns and driveways against general mess and damage.

Miscellaneous
Some projects in this book, especially the Classic Round Pond and the Waterspout, use a wider range of materials than shown here. Specialty materials such as geotextile and butyl may not be available at your DIY superstore. Look up suppliers in a directory of businesses in your area (geotextile and butyl are sold by suppliers of pond-building materials and water features).

TILES, STONE AND PAVERS

Roof tile

Floor tile

Decorative glazed tile

Clay block paver

Concrete paving slab

Reconstituted stone paving slab

Millstone

Real stone slab

York stone

Roof stone

Real stone block

Cobblestones

Boulder

Pebbles

Tiles

A huge range of tiles is available. Clay roof tiles are traditionally used as a coping to finish the top of brickwork structures and help deflect rainwater away from the structure. Decorative clay tiles, designed specifically for brickwork, can be obtained from specialty suppliers. (Those that display a floral decoration are sometimes known as rose blocks.) Some concrete tiles are described as reconstituted stone, because they are made to look like real clay or stone. Terracotta floor tiles, quarry tiles, brightly colored tiles or patterned glazed tiles can all be incorporated into brickwork to make a decorative design.

Stone

Stone is traditionally combined with brick for decorative effect. Many kinds of real stone are available, but it is often best to choose a type that is quarried in your area, because it will harmonize with the color of local bricks. See what your supplier has in stock and look at local examples of building to help you choose. Avoid stone that looks crumbly or cracked. Try to select pieces that can be used as they stand, in order to avoid having to cut them. (If cutting is necessary, see pages 42–43.)

Cobblestones and pebbles may be bedded in mortar to create a patterned surface that complements brickwork or paving.

Paving slabs

Straightforward concrete paving slabs may be too plain for garden projects, but there are many attractive alternatives. Textured and colored slabs, or reconstituted stone slabs (a mixture of crushed stone and concrete) can look as good as real stone. Real stone paving slabs are wonderful, but extremely expensive, so your budget may not be able to accommodate them.

Pavers

You can use ordinary bricks for paving (to match nearby brickwork), but the cavities (frogs or holes) will need to be filled with sand and the bricks cannot be laid with equal gaps between them, because their proportions are designed to incorporate mortar joints—however, this sometimes adds to their charm.

Pavers (or paviors) are extremely hard, thin clay or concrete bricks designed specifically for paths, patios and drives. They come in many shapes, sizes and finishes. Perhaps the most attractive and durable option is the kiln-fired, brick-sized clay paver, in subtle colors that never fade. (Concrete pavers fade in color after five to ten years.) Pavers are exactly twice as long as they are wide, and are usually thinner than a brick, which makes them easier to lay in patterns. The recess required to lay them is shallower than that needed for bricks. Concrete pavers include imitation stone setts (small rectangular paving blocks), and mock bricks.

FOUNDATIONS

When it comes to building foundations, you can't cut costs. Most projects need a solid, no-nonsense concrete foundation. If you suspect that the conditions in your garden mean that a stronger than average foundation is required, adjustments to the basic foundation can be made. For example, if the ground is soft, simply make the foundation wider and deeper, or if the ground is very wet, lay extra hardcore to increase drainage.

ABOUT FOUNDATIONS

Every brickwork project requires a foundation of some kind. A foundation is a strong, stable, level base on which to build. It would be no good laying bricks directly on the ground, because their weight, together with rainwater, would compress and erode the soil causing the brick structure to sink, crack, lean over and fall apart. So whether you are constructing a wall, a birdbath or a patio, start by building a good foundation. Foundations are usually made from hardcore topped by concrete. Foundations for patios and paths often omit the concrete and substitute other materials. Sometimes it is possible to use an existing foundation (see page 35).

TYPES OF FOUNDATION

Most brickwork walls, and upright structures such as barbecues and planters, need a strong hardcore and concrete foundation as illustrated at right.

For paving projects—patios and paths—the foundation can consist of hardcore and a dryish mix of concrete or, alternatively, hardcore and compacted layers of other materials (although not as solid as concrete, this foundation is adequate for domestic patios and paths, and less work to make). This alternative foundation can be made of hardcore, gravel and sand; hardcore and ballast; or hardcore, ballast and sand. In each case, the hardcore, ballast and sand are compacted. However, if the ground is soft, sandy or boggy, it is better to include concrete in the foundation. Also, if the design of the project means that it will be awkward to use the plate compacter required for compacting the materials, opt for a concrete foundation. Edging bricks or blocks need to be stuck down with mortar or contained by a curb.

Backfilling: To fill or pack a cavity (behind a wall or in a foundation trench hole) with earth in order to bring the ground up to the desired level.

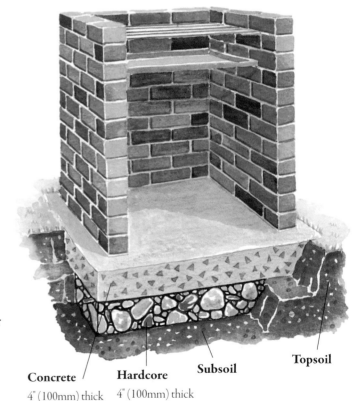

Concrete
4" (100mm) thick

Hardcore
4" (100mm) thick

Subsoil

Topsoil

ABOVE For a tall, weighty structure such as this barbecue, a generous slab of concrete has been set on compacted hardcore.

On Firm Ground

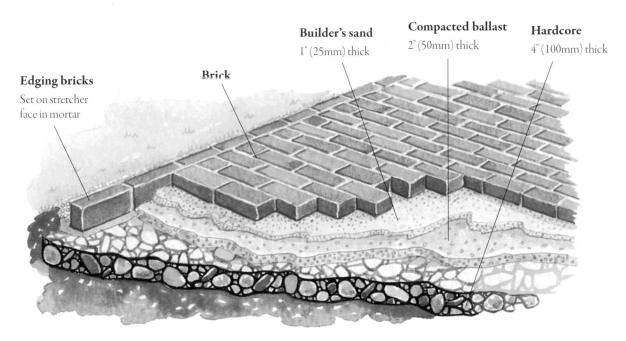

Edging bricks
Set on stretcher
face in mortar

Brick

Builder's sand
1" (25mm) thick

Compacted ballast
2" (50mm) thick

Hardcore
4" (100mm) thick

ABOVE A foundation for a brick patio on firm, well-drained ground. On a patio
with a large area, a plate compacter is used to compress the layers.

On Soft Ground

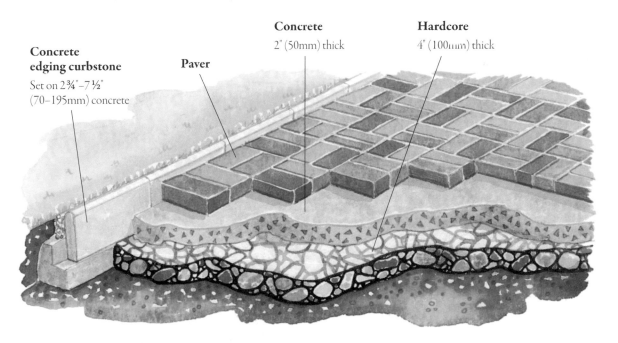

**Concrete
edging curbstone**
Set on 2¾"–7½"
(70–195mm) concrete

Paver

Concrete
2" (50mm) thick

Hardcore
4" (100mm) thick

ABOVE A foundation for a paver patio on moist, soft ground. The thickness of the
hardcore should be increased to 8" (203mm) if water is moving across the site.

MEASURING, MARKING AND DIGGING

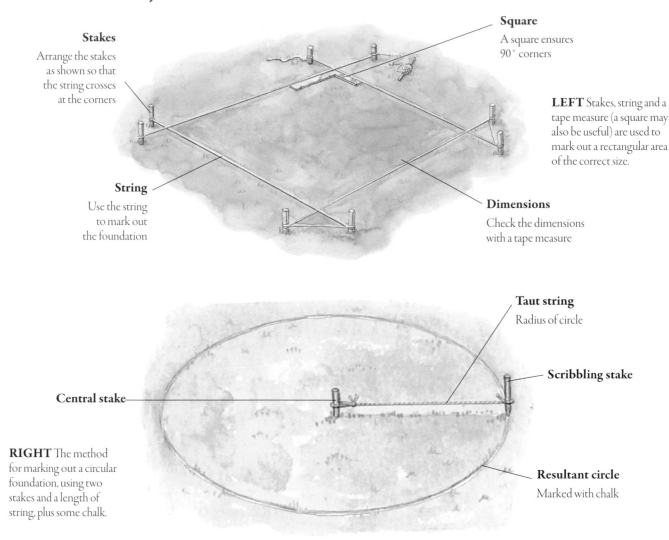

Stakes
Arrange the stakes as shown so that the string crosses at the corners

Square
A square ensures 90° corners

LEFT Stakes, string and a tape measure (a square may also be useful) are used to mark out a rectangular area of the correct size.

String
Use the string to mark out the foundation

Dimensions
Check the dimensions with a tape measure

Taut string
Radius of circle

Central stake

Scribbling stake

RIGHT The method for marking out a circular foundation, using two stakes and a length of string, plus some chalk.

Resultant circle
Marked with chalk

Marking out: Using string, stakes and a tape measure to variously set out the area of a foundation on the ground. Also to mark an individual brick in readiness for cutting.

Work out the exact size of the foundation (for example, although a patio foundation is the same size as the finished patio, a wall foundation needs to be wider than a wall) and its precise depth. To establish the depth, survey the site (if the ground slopes, pound a stake in the ground to indicate the chosen finished level of the foundation) and draw a cross-section of the construction (visualize the project sliced across the middle with a knife) to help calculate the depth of soil that should be removed.

Mark out rectangular areas using stakes, string and a tape measure. If the foundation is an L-shape or other complex shape, divide it into a series of rectangles. To check the accuracy of a rectangle, make sure the opposite sides are of equal length, then measure the diagonals, add them together and divide by two. This tells you how long a diagonal should be in a shape with 90° corners. To make the diagonals equal, adjust the stakes' positions.

For circular foundations, pound a stake into the ground at the center. Make a length of string with a loop at each end (the length from loop to loop should be the same as the radius of the circle). Slip one loop over the central stake, insert another stake into the other end and use it to scribe out a circle. Mark the circle using spray paint, chalk powder or chalk. Dig out the foundation as described on page 22.

LAYING FOUNDATIONS

The initial layer of most foundations consists of hardcore, which is broken and compacted with a sledgehammer to make a firm base. The second layer of a foundation for upright structures, such as a wall or barbecue, is usually concrete. Wooden formwork is normally laid to contain it. Stakes are nailed to the outer side of boards and pounded through the hardcore into the ground, so that they are level with each other. The boards indicate where the top of the concrete should be. When the concrete is laid, a length of wood is used to scrape away excess concrete and tamp it level. For many paving projects, the second layer might consist of gravel, followed by a layer of sand compacted to just below the finished level of the foundation. This is topped with loose sand. (For foundations larger then 10' (3m) in either direction, divide up the area with extra boards set to the finished height of the foundation.)

Formwork
Wooden boards are used to set the level of the concrete

Concrete
The concrete is cast to the level of the boards

> **Compacting:** Using a sledgehammer or the weight of the body to press down a layer of sand, earth or hardcore.

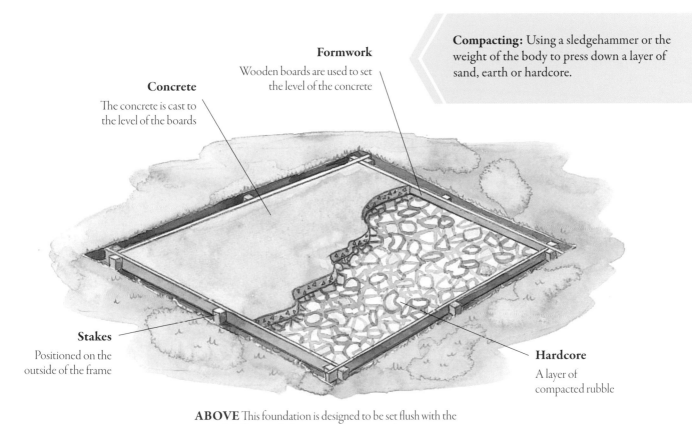

Stakes
Positioned on the outside of the frame

Hardcore
A layer of compacted rubble

ABOVE This foundation is designed to be set flush with the ground. A formwork frame is used to contain the concrete.

USING EXISTING FOUNDATIONS

If a brickwork feature is small, it is sometimes possible to build it on an existing area of paving. Before you do that, if possible check what is underneath the paving by lifting a few bricks, blocks or slabs. If the foundation looks bad, lift the paving in the area you need to build on, dig out extra earth and make an acceptable foundation, replacing the original paving afterwards. Once you are satisfied that the area is solid, check that it is level. Small discrepancies can be compensated for by adding extra mortar under the first course of bricks. If the slope is too great (more than ⅜" (10mm) across the length of the brickwork), cast a level concrete slab on top, no less than 1½" (40mm) thick, on which to build.

CONCRETE AND MORTAR

Concrete and mortar are two very important components in brickwork construction. Concrete is used in foundations and mortar is used to stick bricks together, and for rendering. They are both made from mixing dry ingredients, including cement powder, with water. For successful mixtures, it is important to get the right ratio of ingredients and correct amount of water. For the most part, you can use a shovel to measure out dry ingredients.

ABOUT CONCRETE AND MORTAR

At first, you may look at a concrete or mortar mix and wonder how it is going to work, but it will set solid overnight and gain strength slowly over a few days. Mortar needs to be soft and buttery, so that it slices and cuts, and stays where it has been put without oozing or dribbling. However, the exact consistency required will depend on the absorbency of the bricks, and the humidity of the weather on the day. As with baking the perfect loaf, follow the recipe to the letter, but be ready to make adjustments to suit changing needs. If the weather is dry, spray the bricks and mortar with a fine mist of water as you work.

MIXING METHODS FOR CONCRETE AND MORTAR

For quantities that require in excess of 55 lbs. (25kg) of cement powder, we recommend that you rent a cement mixer.

Mixing in a wheelbarrow

1. Use a shovel to measure out the dry ingredients into the wheelbarrow—first the sand or ballast, and then the cement. Continue until you have enough or the barrow is half-full. Turn the ingredients over several times until they are thoroughly mixed.

2. Pour about one-third of a bucket of water into one end of the wheelbarrow, then drag small amounts of the dry ingredients into the water. Repeat the process until all the water has been soaked up by the dry ingredients.

3. Turn over the whole heap several times, all the while adding small amounts of water, until you can chop it into clean, wet slices.

Mixing
Drag the dry materials into the water

ABOVE It is often convenient to use a wheelbarrow for mixing mortar; remember to give it a good cleaning afterwards.

Mixing on a board

1. Measure the dry ingredients onto a board with a shovel—first the sand or ballast, then the cement. Mix until it is an even color.

Curing time: The time taken for mortar or concrete to become firm and stable. "Part-cured" means that the mortar or concrete is firm enough to bear a small amount of weight.

2. Dig a hole in the center and pour in about half a bucket of water. Work around the heap, dragging small amounts of the dry materials into the water. If the water threatens to break over the rim, swiftly pull in more of the dry materials to stem the flow.

3. When the water has been soaked up, add more until the concrete or mortar is the correct consistency. The finished mixture should form crisp, firm slices that stand up under their own weight without crumbling.

CAUTION

Cement and lime are corrosive and can seriously burn the skin. Always wear goggles and gloves, and wash your hands and face after working with them.

Mixing

Make a hole in the heap and add a small amount of water

ABOVE When mixing on a board, drag the dry materials into the water in the center of the heap. Try not to let the water escape.

Tamping: The act of using a length of wood to compact and level wet concrete.

Floating: The procedure of using a metal, plastic or wooden float to skim wet concrete or mortar to a smooth and level finish.

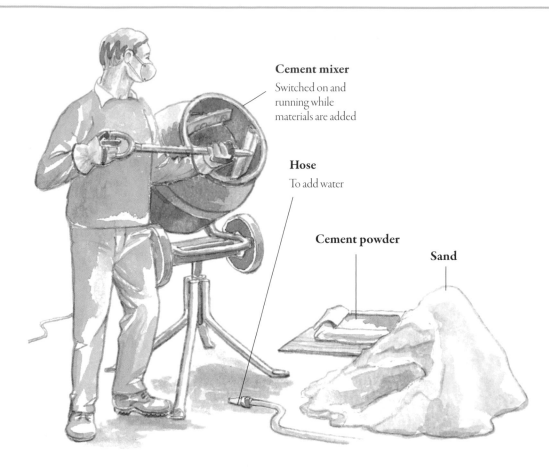

Cement mixer
Switched on and running while materials are added

Hose
To add water

Cement powder

Sand

ABOVE Use a shovel to measure quantities, for example one shovelful (1 part) of cement powder to four shovelfuls (4 parts) of sand.

Mixing using a cement mixer

Follow the instructions supplied with the machine and use an in-line GFCI between the plug and socket. Measure out the sand or ballast using a shovel, switch on the mixer and put it straight into the machine. Don't overfill: a small machine can take about 10–12 shovelfuls (including cement powder). Add the cement. After a few minutes, when the ingredients are evenly mixed, start adding water a little at a time, until the correct consistency is achieved. (See recipes on facing page.)

GENERAL HANDLING OF CONCRETE AND MORTAR

It is best to use buckets to move a small quantity of concrete or mortar, and a wheelbarrow for large amounts. Make sure that the load is balanced. Two half-buckets are easier to move than one bucket that is full to overflowing. The same

goes for a wheelbarrow: it's easier to move two small loads than it is to move a barrow that is so full that it slops and spills when you jolt over a bump. In most instances, a shovel is the best tool for unloading your cargo, although a small spade is good for filling up buckets.

WEATHER CONDITIONS

Concrete and mortar like to cure (see page 37) slowly—the longer the better. If the weather is anything other than cool and damp, then to a lesser or greater extent you need to protect both concrete and mortar. If you have just built a wall and it's so hot that you can see the mortar drying out, cover it with damp newspaper. If the sun is blazing down on newly-laid concrete, cover it with wet burlap and spray it at regular intervals over the next day or so. If you are expecting a night frost, cover both concrete and mortar with dry burlap, layers of newspaper or sheets of plastic. If it starts to rain heavily, cover everything with sheets of plastic.

CONCRETE AND MORTAR RECIPES

Ingredients are measured by volume (in the projects, weights are given only as a guide to ordering materials, since volumes of different materials vary in weight, and sand and ballast are heavier when wet). "Parts" signify the ratios of ingredients (by volume) to each other, measured in the same manner (such as by the shovelful). So a recipe listing 1 part cement and 4 parts sand means 1 shovelful of cement and 4 shovelfuls of sand, or 2 shovelfuls of cement and 8 shovelfuls of sand, depending on the quantity you are mixing. Recipes do vary, but we recommend that you use the following proportions.

Concrete for foundations

1 part cement   4 parts ballast

Mix 1 part cement with 4 parts ballast. Add water and mix to the consistency of stiff mashed potatoes. You can substitute 2 parts coarse sand and 3 parts aggregate for the 4 parts ballast. (You may wish to do this if you have bought these materials in bulk and want to use them instead of ordering ballast.)

Dryish mix of concrete for paving foundations

As above, except that a lot less water is added—just enough to damp down the dry ingredients. The mixture will absorb moisture from the air and set after a few days.

Mortar for bricklaying and pointing

1 part cement   4 parts builder's sand

Mix 1 part cement with 4 parts builder's sand. Add water and mix to the consistency of mashed potatoes. For exposed sites where strong winds and heavy rain may erode the mortar, 1 part cement and 3 parts sand is commonly used.

Dryish mix of mortar for paving joints

As above, except a lot less water is added (add water as described for dryish mix of concrete).

CUTTING BRICK, STONE AND CONCRETE

In many ways, the sign of a good brickworker is the ability to place bricks for best fit without having to cut many of them. When you do need to make a cut, it must be accurate. For the most part, you will be using a club hammer and brick chisel to cut bricks into halves and quarters. To cut concrete slabs and tiles, it might be necessary to use a power angle grinder. Clay tiles can be cut with a heavy-duty ceramic tile cutter.

CUTTING BRICKS

Cutting bricks with a bricklayer's trowel or bricklayer's hammer

The most basic way of cutting a brick is with a bricklayer's trowel: hold the brick in one hand and strike it firmly with the edge of the trowel. If you are lucky, the brick will fall in half. If it doesn't, repeat the procedure on the other face.

To use a bricklayer's hammer, simply hold the brick in one hand—so that the waste end is pointing away from your body—and then use the chisel end of the bricklayer's hammer to chip away at the excess until you have cut back to the mark. Work little by little, backing up to the line of cut.

HOW TO AVOID TOO MUCH CUTTING

- Plan the length and width of the structure—path or wall— so that it is made up from a number of whole bricks.
- If you are using a mixture of materials—such as bricks and tiles, or bricks and concrete slabs—make sure that the module sizes of each are compatible.
- Avoid using a mixture of standard and metric bricks, unless there is a good reason to do so.
- Choose a bond that works without the need to cut bricks.
- Go for structures that are rectilinear in plan view, rather than triangular or hexagonal, for example.
- If you want to use a bond that requires bricks to be cut, at least choose one that only requires you to cut bricks in half.

Pecking: Using the edge of a large trowel or the chisel end of a bricklayer's hammer to nibble the ragged edge of a part-cut brick back to a marked line.

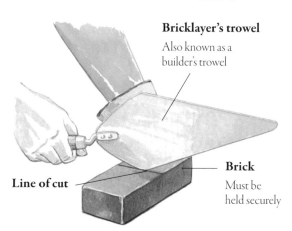

Bricklayer's trowel
Also known as a builder's trowel

Brick
Must be held securely

Line of cut

ABOVE Give the brick a firm, well-placed blow with the edge of the bricklayer's trowel and it should fall in two.

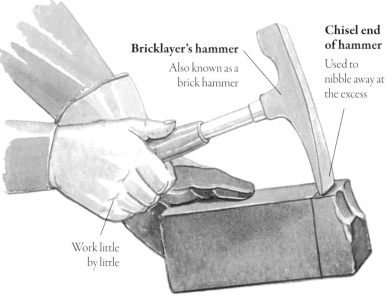

Chisel end of hammer
Used to nibble away at the excess

Bricklayer's hammer
Also known as a brick hammer

Work little by little

ABOVE Work with a pecking action, gradually nibbling back the brick to the marked line of cut.

Cutting bricks with a brick chisel

A more accurate way of cutting bricks is by using a club hammer and brick chisel. This is the method used most frequently in small brickwork projects. Position the brick on something soft, such as a pad of old carpet, or on the lawn, to help absorb the shock of the blow. Wear goggles and strong leather gloves. Take the brick chisel in one hand and the club hammer in the other, and set the edge of the chisel firmly on the line of cut, so that it is upright and square with the brick. Finally, give the chisel a single, well-placed blow with the hammer and the brick should fall in half. It may be wise to practice on some old bricks first.

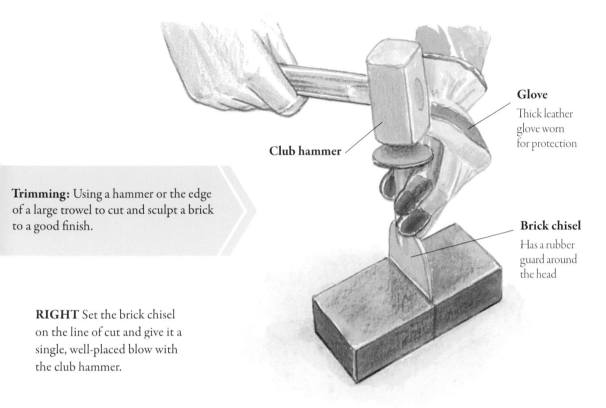

Club hammer

Glove
Thick leather glove worn for protection

Brick chisel
Has a rubber guard around the head

Trimming: Using a hammer or the edge of a large trowel to cut and sculpt a brick to a good finish.

RIGHT Set the brick chisel on the line of cut and give it a single, well-placed blow with the club hammer.

Cutting bricks with a machine

Machines are potentially dangerous—follow the manufacturer's instructions carefully and always wear goggles, a dust mask and gloves. Earmuffs and thick boots are also recommended. There are various machines you can use to cut bricks:

- Angle grinder fitted with a stone-cutting disc (see page 24).
- Brick guillotine. To use a guillotine cutter, mark the brick where you want to cut it and place it on the platform below the chisel-like blade. Pull down on the lever.
- Disc cutter fitted with a stone cutting disc (a disc cutter normally describes a large angle grinder). To use, follow the instructions for an angle grinder (see page 43).
- Circular saw fitted with a masonry blade (handheld power tool). Use in the same way as an angle grinder.
- Masonry saw. To use a masonry saw, place the machine on a level surface, set the brick on the platform, so that the line of cut is aligned with the marking guide, and then pull down on the lever so that the disc makes the cut.

CUTTING TILES, STONE AND CONCRETE

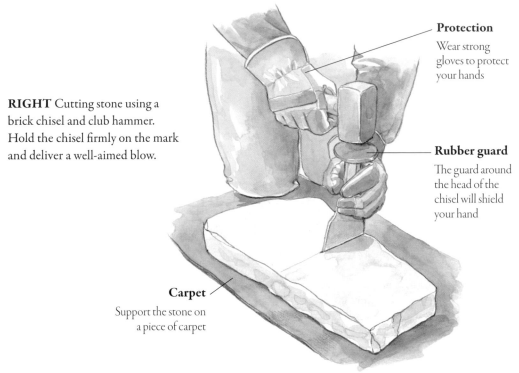

RIGHT Cutting stone using a brick chisel and club hammer. Hold the chisel firmly on the mark and deliver a well-aimed blow.

Protection
Wear strong gloves to protect your hands

Rubber guard
The guard around the head of the chisel will shield your hand

Carpet
Support the stone on a piece of carpet

Tiles

Clay tiles—roof tiles and quarry tiles—are best cut with a good-quality, heavy-duty ceramic tile cutter. All you do is butt the tile hard up against the stop, so that the line of cut is aligned with the handle, and then push the lever forward so that the little wheel scores the surface of the tile. Then you pull the lever back so that the anvil is bridged over the tile, and push down hard so that the tile snaps in half. Clear the debris after every cut.

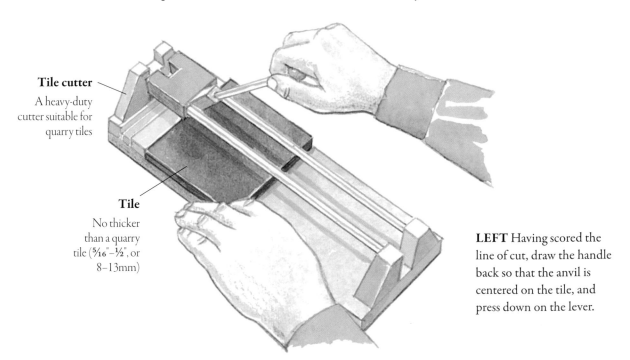

Tile cutter
A heavy-duty cutter suitable for quarry tiles

Tile
No thicker than a quarry tile ($5/16$"–$1/2$", or 8–13mm)

LEFT Having scored the line of cut, draw the handle back so that the anvil is centered on the tile, and press down on the lever.

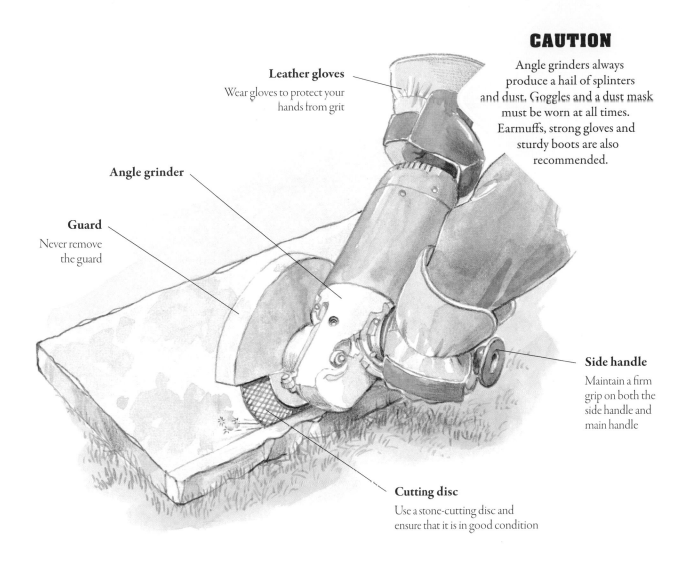

CAUTION

Angle grinders always produce a hail of splinters and dust. Goggles and a dust mask must be worn at all times. Earmuffs, strong gloves and sturdy boots are also recommended.

Leather gloves
Wear gloves to protect your hands from grit

Angle grinder

Guard
Never remove the guard

Side handle
Maintain a firm grip on both the side handle and main handle

Cutting disc
Use a stone-cutting disc and ensure that it is in good condition

ABOVE Hold the grinder firmly, and keeping your body well away from the line of cut, make repeated light passes to cut a groove.

Cutting stone and concrete with an angle grinder

Set the slab flat on the lawn and use a tape measure and chalk to draw out the line of cut. Put on goggles, a dust mask, earmuffs and gloves. Hold the grinder so that the wheel is at right angles to the slab. Brace yourself, switch on the power and gently run the spinning disc forward, to lightly score along the marked cut. Make several runs to deepen the line of cut, then switch off the power and flip the slab over.

Switch the power back on and re-run the whole procedure on the other side. Continue repeating the process until the slab of stone or concrete falls in two. During the whole cutting operation, always make sure that both you and the power cord remain well clear of the cutting disc. Always use an in-line GFCI.

BRICKLAYING

There can be something truly calming and therapeutic about bricklaying. The trick is to make sure that everything is well prepared, with the piles of bricks comfortably within reach, and the mortar at the ready, so that your rhythm of work is not broken. It is perfectly possible to cope with the work on your own, but if you can find a willing helper to pile up the bricks and mix the mortar, so much the better.

PLANNING THE COURSES

Walls and box structures

To build a wall, allow ⅜" (10mm) between each brick for mortar, and lay out a line of bricks to fit your chosen measurement in the best way. (If you are building a box structure, measure out the next side and repeat the procedure already described.) Lay the second course on the first so that the vertical joints are staggered. Working in this way, you will be able to plan out the structure without the need to cut bricks.

Coursing: Part of the process of bricklaying—bedding a number of bricks on a bed of mortar in order to build a course (a horizontal layer of bricks).

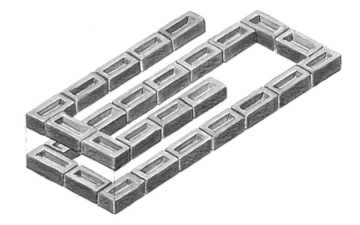

ABOVE Plan out the initial two courses of a box structure first.

Circles, curves and arches

Let's say that you want to build a circle or curve of bricks with a 3' 3" (1m) radius. Take two wooden stakes and link them with string, so that they are 3' 3" (1m) apart. Pound one stake in the ground, and use the other stake to indicate the circle (see page 34). Lay the bricks (dry) around the circumference of the circle. When you come to the last brick, make adjustments to the gaps between each brick in the whole circle, to achieve a good fit. (The fit of the bricks can be planned on a scaled drawing, if you wish.) You may like to consider using half-bricks, or bricks laid on their stretcher (side) face, to create curved structures. If you are building an arch, plan it out on the ground before you start work, in order to avoid mistakes.

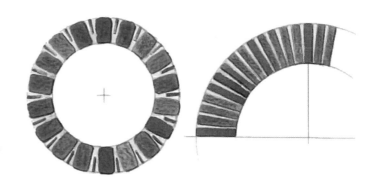

ABOVE Half-bricks with tiles (left) and bricks set on edge (right).

BASIC PROCEDURES

RIGHT Set the brick carefully in place on the mortar and tap it level with the handle of the bricklayer's trowel.

Bedding: The process of pressing a brick, slab or stone into a bed or layer of wet mortar and ensuring that it is level.

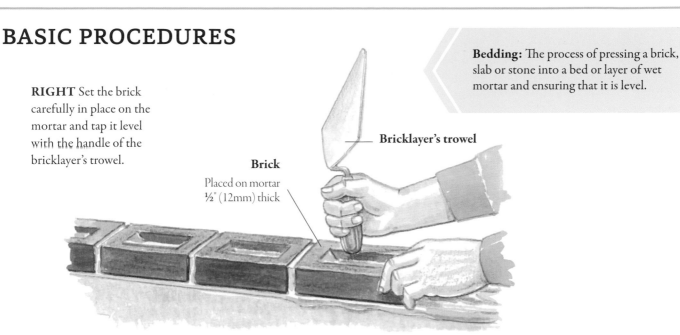

Bricklayer's trowel

Brick
Placed on mortar
½" (12mm) thick

Setting out the line

Determine the line of the wall by pounding in a stake at each end of the concrete foundation. Take a length of string and run it over a piece of chalk, or through a container of chalk powder. Stretch the line between the stakes, a few millimeters above the ground, tying it so that it is taut and flush with the ground. When you are happy that the line is marking the course of the wall, lift it between finger and thumb and let it go with a snap, so that it slaps down a line of chalk on the concrete. (Alternatively, use a simple device called a chalk line, containing replaceable chalk, which deposits chalk on a string as you pull it out of the container.)

RIGHT There are several ways to apply mortar—this is just one of them. It is a good method for beginners.

Mortar
Excess mortar pushed on to end of brick

Bricklayer's trowel

Line checked with level

Buttering: The act of using a trowel during bricklaying to cover some part of a brick with wet mortar, prior to setting it in position on a bed of mortar.

Applying mortar

Spread a line of mortar about ½" (12mm) thick and 12" (30cm) long, and draw the point of the trowel through it to make a valley. Set the first brick in place and tap it with the handle of the trowel so that the excess squeezes out, and the mortar joint is about ⅜" (10mm) thick. Use the point of the trowel to push the excess mortar up on to the end of the brick to form the vertical joint, and then lay the second brick. Continue in this way until the end of the row. Check each course for height, and use the level vertically, horizontally and diagonally to check that all the bricks are in line (see page 20).

ADDITIONAL TECHNIQUES

If you are finding it difficult to keep a uniform thickness of mortar between the joints when building a wall, a gauge rod will help. In effect, this is a batten marked off along its length with alternate thicknesses for bricks and joints—2½" (65mm) for the height or thickness of the brick, ⅜" (10mm) for the thickness of the mortar, then 2½" (65mm), ⅜" (10mm), 2½" (65mm) and so on along the batten (measure the thickness of your bricks first). Simply stand this against the wall being built and use it to assess your progress, then make necessary adjustments by knocking the bricks harder or by adding more mortar.

Never assume that you can make mistakes here and there and make good at the end—you can't. It is important to be consistent and make sure that every brick is placed well.

USING A TRAMMEL

A trammel is used when building circles or circle-based curves. It usually consists of a length of wood (trammel arm) drilled at one end, a block of wood the thickness of a brick (trammel support block), and a sheet of plywood (base). The support block is positioned on the base, surrounded by bricks to keep it in place. The trammel arm pivots on a nail hammered into the trammel support block. Each brick is placed so that it is aligned with the center of the circle, and so that it just touches the end of the arm. A U-shaped piece may be attached to the arm to indicate the position of the edge bricks, which are laid to meet the end of the trammel at 90°. There are also slightly different versions of the trammel.

Trammel arm

Trammel support block

ABOVE If desired, a nail can be attached to the arm as a pointer.

Watering: Wetting bricks at the start of a work session, prior to bedding them on mortar.

THINGS TO AVOID

- On a hot day, don't use bricks dry: always dampen them so that they feel slightly less absorbent to the touch.
- Don't immediately scrape off excess mortar as it oozes out from between the bricks, because you will stain the bricks. It is much better to leave it until the bricks have absorbed the water from the mortar, and then scrape it off with the trowel.
- Don't use coarse sand, dirty sand or stale cement to make mortar; use builder's sand and fresh cement.
- Don't let the mortar on the trowels and level dry out—wash them every half hour or so.

POINTING

"Pointing" describes the finishing of the mortar joint between the bricks. There are four common finishes: raked or keyed, mason's, flat or flush, and weathered or struck. Pointing is done as the bricks are laid (avoid if the mortar is wet and sloppy), or when the wall is complete.

Raked joints are created by using a round bar, trowel handle or another tool to run along the joint in order to hollow it. When using old bricks to build walls in the garden, the best finish is a raked joint: wait until the end of the day, and then use the point of the pointing trowel to swiftly rake the joint clear of excess mortar. This finish is perfect for a rustic garden wall.

A mason's joint is formed by wiping the mortar into a peak. Flush joints are made by using the edge of the trowel to scrape the mortar off flush with the bricks. In a weathered joint, the mortar is scraped out at an angle.

Raking out: Using a trowel to rake out some part of the mortar from between courses, so that the edges of the bricks are clearly and crisply revealed.

Raked or keyed joint

Mason's joint

Flat or flush joint

Weathered or struck joint

Pointing: Using a trowel, stick or a tool of your choice to bring mortar joints to the desired finish.

LEFT The joints between bricks need to be filled neatly with mortar. Use the edge of the trowel to wipe the mortar into the joint. Approach from both sides in order to create a peaked effect (mason's joint).

INCORPORATING OTHER MATERIALS

In times past, brick walls were traditionally less uniform affairs, with bricks of varying thickness and much thicker joints. In some areas, it was common to stud wide joints with little pieces of stone or broken tiles. Rather than going to the trouble of cutting or rubbing bricks to create shaped bricks for arches, it was quite usual to use a stack of roof tiles or old quarry tiles to fill the space. In some coastal areas, it was common to stud joints with shells. Some builders incorporated specially shaped bricks.

BRICK BONDS AND PATTERNS

The pattern created by placing bricks to form a continuous wall, or laying them to form a patio surface, is known as the bond. The secret of creating a sound brick wall lies in the vertical joints of neighboring courses—these must be staggered. If vertical joints are not staggered, the structural integrity of the brickwork is at risk. There are various traditional bonds that achieve this. Look around your area for examples of brick patterns.

BASIC BONDS FOR WALLS AND STRUCTURES

The three primary bonds are running bond, English bond and Flemish bond. In a running bond, also known as a stretcher bond, each course is formed entirely of stretchers (side face of the brick), and it is only suitable for walls 4" (10.25cm)—half a brick—thick. Each brick half-laps half its length on the bricks in the course below. A running bond is great when you only want to build a low structure or a cavity wall.

In an English bond, alternate courses show headers (end face of the brick, see page 27) and stretchers. The end or head of the brick is centered on the middle of the stretcher in the course below.

Flemish bond consists of alternate headers and stretchers in each course, with headers always being placed over the center of the stretcher below. Less common bonds are shown below.

Running or stretcher bond

English bond

Flemish bond

SPECIAL BONDS

English garden wall bond

Heading bond

Flemish garden wall bond

Honeycomb bond

PATTERNS

Patterns on walls

Different colored bricks can be used to create a pattern, as in the English diaper tradition (an all-over surface decoration of a small repeated pattern such as diamonds or squares, using colored, projecting or recessed bricks).

The way bricks are arranged can also create a pattern—either a self-pattern, as with a herringbone panel, or together with tiles.

Diaper pattern (darker color)

Diaper pattern (lighter color)

Patterns on patios and paths

Patterns for patios and paths are created in much the same way as for walls, by brick color or arrangement. Because there are not the same concerns about structural integrity as for a wall, you can introduce additional elements, such as stones and shells, to create patterns, or use different thicknesses of brick.

Herringbone band course

Raking tile courses

WALLS AND OTHER STRUCTURES

Brick walls are all around us—but next time you are out walking, notice how arches, columns, piers and pillars can be used to lift a structure out of the ordinary, with a unique coming together of beauty and function. At its most basic, a brick wall can be one brick thick, just two or three courses high, and built on an existing foundation. For a wall like this, the first course of bricks would just be bedded on mortar and the bricks cut to fit.

CONSTRUCTING WALLS

Supporting piers and buttresses

If you are building a freestanding wall from scratch, over three courses high, it needs a foundation of compacted hardcore and a concrete slab, and piers about every 2 yds (2m). If it is two bricks thick, the piers are adequate, but if you want to cut costs and build a single-brick-thick wall, supporting buttresses will also be needed about every 1 yd (1m).

Corners and junctions

Corners and junctions are created by changing the direction of the bricks, arranging them in such a way that the corner or junction can be achieved without changing the bond. Right angles are the easiest to achieve.

Sloping sites

If the slope is gentle, dig a deep trench, lay a concrete slab below ground level, then build the wall. But if the slope is extreme, dig the trench and construct a stepped concrete slab (all below ground), making the concrete risers the same thickness as a brick (see lower illustration).

Curved walls

If the curve is big enough, the bricks can be nudged slightly so that the vertical joints open up and allow the bricks to run around the curve. But if the curve is tight, the easiest option is to either use half-bricks—like building an arch—or to stand the bricks on edge and build the wall from soldier courses.

Coping

A coping functions like a hat—it throws rain away from the face of the wall and keeps it from soaking into the wall. It also has a decorative purpose—it is a way of finishing off the wall and making it pleasing to the eye.

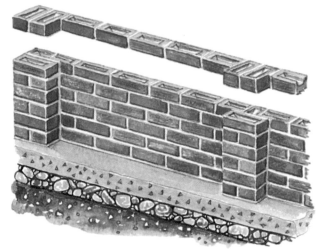

ABOVE A single-brick wall, with piers at regular intervals.

Sighting: To judge by eye whether or not a cut, joint or structure is level or true. To look down or along a wall in order to determine whether or not the structure is level.

ABOVE A wall that runs up a slope needs a stepped foundation.

OTHER STRUCTURES

Box structures
Plan the bond so that the bricks can be run from side to corner, and from corner to side, without being cut.

Columns and pillars
The simplest freestanding column or pillar can be merely a brick square, with the bricks turned 90° in neighboring courses, and each course showing either a stretcher or a pair of headers (opposite left). However, the best option is to go for a pillar that has a stretcher alongside a header in every course (opposite right).

Arches
In backyard brickwork, arches are best built either from half-bricks, or from bricks that run through the thickness of the wall. Either way, the bricks are placed so that the stretcher (side) or header (end) face of the brick is looking to the inside of the arch.

ABOVE A minimal, two-by-two pillar for rough work.

ABOVE A four-by-four pillar for top-quality work.

ABOVE AND BELOW Whole bricks running on their stretcher face.

ABOVE A single-brick-thick wall with an arch made of half-bricks.

PATIOS, PATHS AND STEPS

Patios, paths and steps are an essential part of everyday life. If you need one of these structures for your garden, what better way of making it than by laying a pattern of bricks. Whether you are planning a patio outside the back door, a functional path running the length of the garden, or a very short decorative step up to the front door, bricks will do the job beautifully. Old bricks have a special character and charm.

CONSTRUCTING PATIOS AND PATHS

Patios

A patio always needs a foundation to keep it from sinking, and an edging to keep it from spreading. These need to be equal (in size, structure and permanence) to the composition of the soil, the character of the patio, the combined weight of the materials and to the expected usage. A firm, dry, stony soil requires the minimum of groundwork, but a wet, soft site requires hardcore, concrete and drainage, plus an edging complete with a foundation.

Paths

Because a path gets heavier use than a patio, it needs a deeper foundation and a more permanent edging. The stucture of the edging might need to change over its length depending on the characteristics of the yard that borders it (e.g lawn, flowerbed).

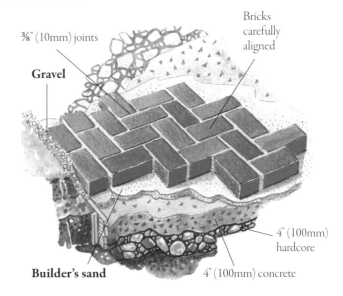

⅜" (10mm) joints · Gravel · Bricks carefully aligned · 4" (100mm) hardcore · 4" (100mm) concrete · Builder's sand

ABOVE A patio foundation with formwork left in place.

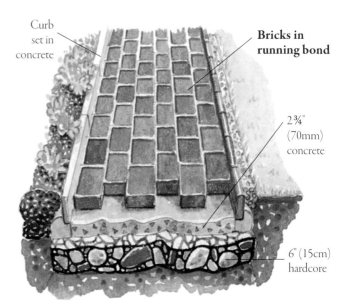

Curb set in concrete · **Bricks in running bond** · 2¾" (70mm) concrete · 6" (15cm) hardcore

ABOVE A path foundation with extra depth of hardcore.

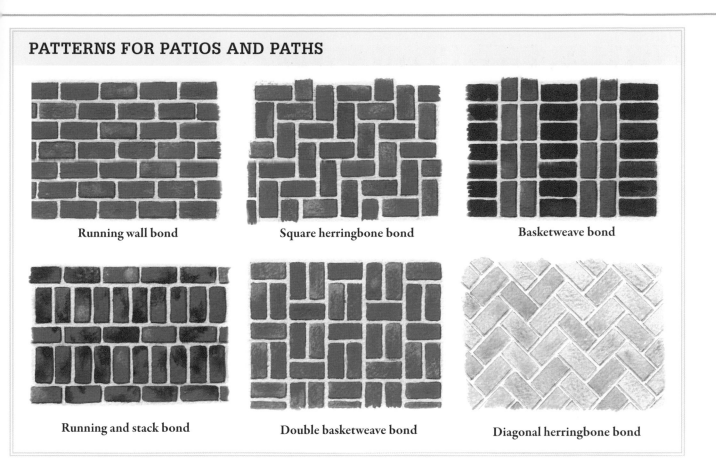

PATTERNS FOR PATIOS AND PATHS

Running wall bond

Square herringbone bond

Basketweave bond

Running and stack bond

Double basketweave bond

Diagonal herringbone bond

CONSTRUCTING STEPS

Steps in the garden

The height (riser measurement) and width of a step are very important. Steps should be no greater than 9" (23cm) high, and no less than 2⅜" (60mm) high (a good average would be 6" (15cm)). The width of the tread should be at least 11¾"–16" (30–40cm), front to back.

A single step on firm ground only needs a foundation of compacted hardcore. If the soil is soft and you want three or more steps, the bottom tread must be built on a firm foundation of 5" (13cm) of compacted hardcore and 5" (13cm) of concrete.

A doorstep gets a lot of use, and needs a firm foundation of 4" (100mm) of compacted hardcore and 4" (100mm) of concrete.

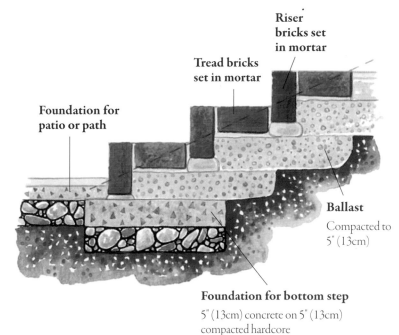

Riser bricks set in mortar

Tread bricks set in mortar

Foundation for patio or path

Ballast Compacted to 5" (13cm)

Foundation for bottom step 5" (13cm) concrete on 5" (13cm) compacted hardcore

ABOVE If you want to ensure that the structure is extra-firm, replicate the foundation for the bottom step under every step (do not use ballast).

FINISHING AND MAINTENANCE

It doesn't take long to transform a pile of bricks, a heap of sand and lots of bags of cement into walls, paths, a patio and other brick structures—all of which need to be finished off and cleaned. Occasionally, the brickwork will also need maintenance. This section shows you how. Remember that by keeping bricks free from plant growth and filling in cavities, you will help prevent frost damage.

CLEANING BRICKWORK AFTER BUILDING

ABOVE Use a wire brush and work diagonally, so that you don't scour mortar out of the joints.

Basic cleaning

If you take care, when laying bricks, not to splash, squirt and smear mortar on the face of the brickwork, there should not be too much cleaning to do. Once the mortar has been allowed to dry overnight, use a stick of wood and a wire brush to knock off, and brush off, occasional splashes of mortar (concentrating on the brick and avoiding the mortar joints).

Chemical cleaning

Some types of brick can be cleaned with a special chemical that is sprayed or brushed on. This should only be used if recommended by the manufacturer of the bricks you are using, since it is possible to damage brickwork if used on the wrong type of brick.

Salts and efflorescence

A white powdery residue or "salting" may develop on the bricks, depending on type. This can be left, brushed off, or treated with vinegar or a chemical cleaner. On reconstituted stone (concrete products) such as block pavers or slabs, a patchy white effect may appear on the surface. This is normal and referred to as efflorescence. It is temporary but can be removed with special cleaners.

CLEANING: THINGS TO AVOID

- Do not touch mortar when it is still wet; leave it overnight before cleaning.
- Do not let mortar become iron-hard before cleaning.
- Try not to wash away mortar from the joints.
- Do not scrape the surface of the bricks with metal tools.
- Avoid leaving a mortar residue when washing off the bricks.
- Do not use chemicals on brickwork unless recommended by the manufacturer.

Wire brushing: Using a wire-bristled brush to remove dry mortar from the face of bricks, for example on a wall, or the surface of a path or patio.

MAINTAINING BRICKWORK

With brickwork projects, little or no maintenance is expected. Bricks should last several lifetimes; however, there are problems that may occur. Poor-quality bricks can crumble, frost can damage the surface of the bricks, or a brick may crack (cracks usually indicate poor pointing— see below for how to remedy). Mortar can be eroded quickly if the mortar mix was poorly measured out; erosion is also possible after many years, especially when exposed to lots of harsh, wet weather.

Repointing

Repointing is the process of replacing some of the mortar between the bricks, and is necessary when the original mortar has been eroded. Before adding slivers of new mortar, it may first be necessary to rake or chisel out mortar to make an adequate recess of ½"–⅝" (12–15mm) deep. Experiment with a small area first, in order to ensure a good color match. Finish as you would for normal pointing (see page 47).

Replacing bricks

Find a new, matching brick, and use a brick chisel and a club hammer to cut out the damaged brick. Avoid damaging the surrounding bricks by levering with the chisel. Chisel out all the mortar in the recess and brush out the dust. Dampen the bottom and sides of the hole a little, prior to lining with stiff mortar. Put mortar on top of the replacement brick and carefully push it in place. Finish the joints as normal (see page 47).

Reinforcing brickwork

If brickwork in your garden is showing signs of structural failure, you will have to repair it. If the top of a wall is disintegrating, the top few courses need to be relaid and a protective coping added.

If brickwork is cracked or leaning, the foundation is failing. If the problem doesn't look too bad, reinforce or underpin the foundation, bit by bit, with sections of additional concrete, and replace the damaged brickwork. If the wall looks really terrible, demolish it.

PART 2: PROJECTS

FLOWER BORDER EDGING

If your flower borders merge into the lawn, spruce them up with a neat brick edging. This traditional English design, commonly found in Sussex, uses rows of beautiful handmade bricks to form a decorative edge that separates the earth from the lawn. It looks very attractive, especially in a lush garden. Brick edging is also a wonderful timesaver when it comes to mowing the lawn.

 TIME
One weekend per 5 yds (5m) length of edging.

Special Tips

This design is intended for straight borders, but it can also be used for gentle curves (experiment without mortar before you build).

YOU WILL NEED

For an edging 5 yds (5m) long and 10⅝" (27cm) wide

 Materials
- Hardcore: 7 cu. feet (0.2 cu. meters)
- Bricks: 85
- Mortar: 1 part (80 lbs., or 36kg) cement and 4 parts (315 lbs., or 144kg) sand

 Tools
- Tape measure, stakes and string
- Spade and fork
- Wheelbarrow and bucket
- Sledgehammer
- Shovel and mixing board, or cement mixer
- Bricklayer's trowel
- Club hammer
- Brick chisel

BORDER LINES

This design is very practical: the rows of bricks are laid at the same level as the lawn, making it easy to mow (and less work to trim). The lawnmower can be pushed hard up against the zigzag edging that holds back the earth, with its wheels running along the brick track next to it.

There are a number of options you may want to consider before starting. First of all, think about the style of your garden and whether or not this traditional English pattern is suitable. For a more modern look, for example, you could have a single line of black bricks partnered with a line of blue glazed tiles.

This is a very simple project to make and you are unlikely to encounter any problems. In fact, it is an ideal project to begin with if you are new to brickwork.

Cut-Away Detail of the Flower Border Edging

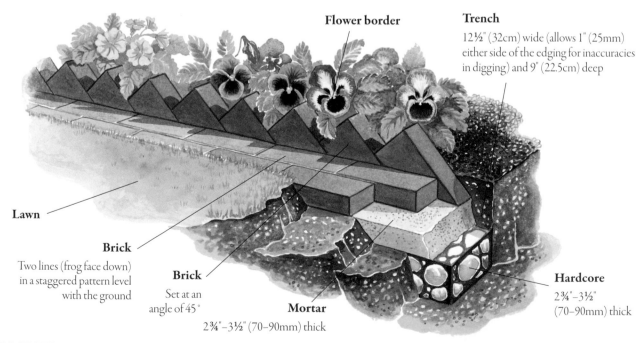

Flower border

Trench
12½" (32cm) wide (allows 1" (25mm) either side of the edging for inaccuracies in digging) and 9" (22.5cm) deep

Lawn

Brick
Two lines (frog face down) in a staggered pattern level with the ground

Brick
Set at an angle of 45°

Mortar
2¾"–3½" (70–90mm) thick

Hardcore
2¾"–3½" (70–90mm) thick

Turf
Remove the turf first and see if it can be used elsewhere in the garden

Digging
Dig out the earth in shallow spadefuls

String
Make sure that the two strings remain taut and parallel

1 Decide where to put the edging (we wanted to increase the width of an existing flower border and avoid damaging plants). Use the stakes and string to mark an area 12½" (32cm) wide (this allows 1" (25mm) either side of the edging for inaccuracies in digging) and as long as your border. Use the spade and fork to remove the turf and dig a trench 9" (22.5cm) deep. Remove the stakes and string.

Hardcore
Systematically break and compact the hardcore until you have a level layer

2 Spread hardcore in the trench and use the sledgehammer to compact it. Break up any pieces larger than half a brick. Continue spreading hardcore, breaking and compacting until you have filled the trench with 2¾"–3½" (70–90mm) of hardcore. Remove any pieces that stick up above this height.

Club hammer
Allow the
weight of the
hammer to do
the work

Flower border
Remove the turf
to extend the
border when the
edging is in place

3 Spread mortar along a 1 yd (1m)-long section of trench, using the bricklayer's trowel, making it 2¾"–3½" (70–90mm) thick. Don't try to do more than 1 yd (1m) at a time. Position two lines of bricks (frog face down) in a staggered pattern and knock them level with the ground using the handle of the club hammer. Use the club hammer and brick chisel to cut half-bricks when needed.

Level
Try to keep the
bricks level with
each other (and
slightly lower
than the level of
the lawn)

Guide
Use the width
of a brick
to ascertain
the depth of
the zigzag

4 Position the angled bricks carefully and tap them into the bed of mortar. Aim for an angle of 45°. You can use another brick as a guide to how far the brick needs to sink down (as shown); alternatively just knock it in so that it appears even. Finish the section; repeat the procedure to complete the edging.

Helpful Hint
After placing about six angled bricks, stand back and check that they are all at 45° and pushed down to the correct depth. If things go wrong, just pull out the offending bricks, add extra mortar and replace them in the correct position.

COUNTRY COTTAGE PATH

One of the best ways of creating a joyous splash of color and pattern in the garden is to build a red brick path in the country cottage tradition. It's a beautifully simple concept that involves gathering as many bricks as you can find—the older and more battered the better—and arranging them in a three-by-three basketweave pattern.

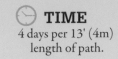

⏱ **TIME**
4 days per 13' (4m) length of path.

Special Tips

You might prefer another brick pattern. See page 49 for alternatives.

YOU WILL NEED

For a path 13' (4m) long and 2' 3" (69cm) wide

 Materials

- Bricks: 186
- Hardcore: 9 cu. feet (0.25 cu. meters)
- Ballast: 550 lbs. (250kg)
- Sand: 550 lbs. (250kg)
- Mortar: 1 part (33 lbs., or 15kg) cement and 4 parts (130 lbs., or 60kg) sand
- Wood for formwork: 26' (8m) of 2" x 4" (40 x 80mm) section
- Wood for stakes: 6 pieces (minimum), 12" (30cm) long, 2" (35mm) wide and 1" (20mm) thick
- Wood for screed board: 1 piece, 2' 3" (69cm) long, 5" (11.5cm) wide and 1" (20mm) thick; 1 piece, 2' 7" (79.5cm) long, 2" (35mm) wide and 1" (20mm) thick
- Nails: 6 (minimum) x 2" (50mm) (formwork), and 2 x 1½" (35mm) (screed board)

 Tools

- Tape measure, stakes and string
- Club hammer
- Spade and fork
- Wheelbarrow and bucket
- Sledgehammer
- General-purpose saw
- Claw hammer
- Plate compacter
- Shovel and mixing board, or cement mixer
- Bricklayer's trowel
- Rake
- Broom

PAVING THE WAY

Many beautiful gardens feature patterned brickwork paths. The warm tones of clay bricks arranged in small-scale, intricate patterns look wonderful, especially on a hazy summer's day when they are set against the fresh tones of foliage and a bright patchwork of flowers.

Various combinations of brick color and layout pattern allow endless design possibilities. This basketweave design will look great in traditional, cottage-type gardens. Most designs entail the same building techniques as this path. The path is ideal for light use and is just the right width to permit a wheelbarrow to be pushed along it. If you need a wider path, let the pattern of bricks dictate the precise width (and avoid cutting bricks as much as possible).

You won't be digging down too deep to make the foundation, so do not worry about exposing pipes leading to and from the house; however, take the usual precautions when siting the path. Check the location of underground utility pipes (gas, water main, drains, oil supplies) and avoid situating a project nearby.

Cut-Away Detail of the Country Cottage Path

Stakes
Nailed to formwork

Formwork
Set level with the ground

Brick edging
Line of bricks set in mortar to be level with formwork

Mortar

Dug-out area
31" (79.5cm) wide and 10" (24.8cm) deep

Basketweave pattern

Additional sand
Added to maintain a recess 4½" (11cm) deep

Sand
½" (15mm) thick

Ballast
1½" (35mm) thick

Hardcore
3" (75mm) thick

Hardcore
Pound into small pieces to form a compact layer

Sledgehammer
Choose a hammer weight to suit your strength

Screed board
Use the board to spread and level the ballast

Path width
The space between the formwork boards should be 2' 3" (69cm)

Stakes
Fixed to outer side of formwork

1 Plan where the path is to go and use the tape measure, club hammer, stakes and string to mark out an area on the ground 31" (79.5cm) wide and as long as required. Dig out the turf and soil to a depth of 10" (24.8cm) using the spade and fork. Spread hardcore in the trench and pound it with a sledgehammer to break up large pieces and form a compacted, level layer 3" (75mm) thick.

2 Nail stakes to the outer side of the formwork and position it in the trench so that it is level with the ground on either side. Test that your bricks fit within the formwork by laying out a small area of pattern. Spread ballast to just above the level of the bottom of the formwork and use the plate compacter to compact it into a layer 1½" (35mm) thick. Make a screed board and scrape away the excess ballast.

Mortar
Scrape away excess mortar

Edging
Set the bricks level with the formwork

3 Mix up some stiff mortar and lay a line of bricks either side of the path, setting them on their stretcher face (side). Do not leave gaps between the bricks. Tap them level with the top of the formwork and use the trowel to scrape away the excess mortar that squeezes out from under the bricks.

Screed board

Recut the board to allow for the ½" (15mm) of sand that has been added

Working action

Use a gentle tapping and dragging action

4 Once the mortar has set, spread a layer of sand and use the plate compacter to compact it into a layer ⅛" (15mm) thick. Avoid vibrating and dislodging the edge bricks. Spread more sand and recut the screed board so that it fits between the rows of edge bricks. Scrape away excess sand to leave a recess, approximately 4½" (11cm) deep, for the rest of the bricks.

Depth

Check the depth of the recess—it needs to be 4½" (11cm)

Size and color

Experiment to find the most attractive arrangement of colors and the best fit

5 Lay the bricks, stretcher face up, in the basketweave pattern. Avoid stepping on the sand. Work from one end to the other and occasionally stand back to check your progress. When all the bricks have been laid, brush sand into the joints. Fix a pad (or piece of carpet) to the plate compacter and run it over the bricks.

Helpful Hint

Because bricks are proportioned to allow for the mortar joints used in bricklaying, the gaps between the bricks at the sides and ends will vary. Compensate for this by distributing them as evenly as possible.

RAISED HERRINGBONE PATIO

The wonderful thing about a patio is that it immediately becomes a focal point, and broadens the way you use the garden. It makes a great surface for a barbecue, the perfect place for a family meal, and a super-safe area for children to play on. If you enjoy doing puzzles, you will like the process of laying the herringbone surface.

 TIME

Three days to prepare the foundation and one day to complete the patio.

Special Tips

A raised patio requires less digging and earth removal than a ground-level patio.

YOU WILL NEED
For a patio 10' (3.02m) square

 Materials
- Bricks: 104 (retaining wall) and 351 (patio surface)
- Hardcore: 26 cu. feet (0.75 cu. meters)
- Ballast: 1 ton
- Sand: 1 ton
- Mortar: 1 part (44 lbs., or 20kg) cement and 4 parts (175 lbs., or 80kg) sand
- Wood for screed board: 1 piece, 9' 10" (3m) long, 6" (15cm) wide and 1" (20mm) thick

Tools
- Tape measure, stakes and string
- Club hammer
- Spade and fork
- Wheelbarrow and bucket
- Shovel and mixing board, or cement mixer
- Sledgehammer
- Bricklayer's trowel and pointing trowel
- Level
- Plate compacter
- Rake
- Brick chisel
- Broom

A PATTERN TO FOLLOW

If you have a small, modern garden, you can adjust this design to make it less quaint—perhaps by inserting contrasting zigzags of stone, inlaid wood or textured metal. Or a variation in the pattern might look nice (see pages 49 and 53), but bear in mind that some patterns require many more bricks to be cut and therefore it will take longer to make the patio.

This concept of a raised patio built within a retaining wall is often chosen in order to minimize the building work involved in a patio project, because less earth needs to be dug out and removed from the site than for a ground-level patio. Even so, remember that building any patio is hard work, and fairly costly because you are usually dealing with a large area. Save up for quality bricks, allocate a few weekends to complete the work, and ask for helpers.

When surveying your site, consider the finished height of the patio in relation to existing doorways, steps or paths. If the patio is to be attached to the house, do not cover air bricks (perforated bricks near the bottom of the walls of the house) and do not build the patio any higher than 6" (15cm) below the damp-proof course of the house. Most importantly, the patio should slope away from the house by 1" (25mm) per 6' 6" (2m).

Cut-Away Detail of the Raised Herringbone Patio

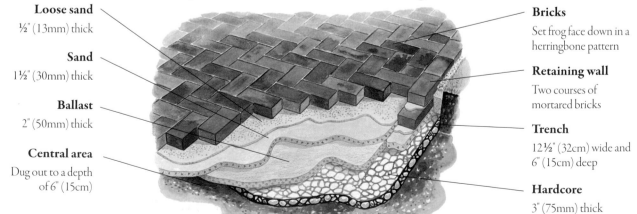

Loose sand
½" (13mm) thick

Sand
1½" (30mm) thick

Ballast
2" (50mm) thick

Central area
Dug out to a depth of 6" (15cm)

Bricks
Set frog face down in a herringbone pattern

Retaining wall
Two courses of mortared bricks

Trench
12½" (32cm) wide and 6" (15cm) deep

Hardcore
3" (75mm) thick

Trench

Dig out to
12½" (32cm)
wide and
6" (15cm) deep

Hardcore

Compact the
hardcore until
it is level and
3" (75mm) thick

Level

Remove stubborn
pieces that
stick out

1 Using the tape measure,
stakes, string and club
hammer, mark out the size and
position of the patio, allowing
an extra 4" (100mm) all around
(10' 4" (3.23m) square). If you are
building against a wall, do not add
on an extra 4" (100mm) on that
side. Check that the patio area is
square (see page 34). Dig a trench
12½" (32cm) wide and 6" (15cm)
deep all around the edge, within
the square. Spread hardcore in
the trench and compact with the
sledgehammer to a finished depth
of 3" (75mm).

Club hammer

Use the handle
of the hammer to
knock the bricks
into position

Wall

Build the wall two
bricks high. On
the top course,
lay the frog
face downwards

2 Build a two-brick-high
retaining wall along the
middle of the trench. Lay the first
course of bricks on a generous
thickness of mortar, leaving
⅜" (10mm)-wide joints between
the bricks. Check that the wall is
straight and level (or sloping away
from your house as appropriate).
Finish the joints with the pointing
trowel (by inserting mortar if
necessary, smoothing, scraping
away and creating a slight dip
between the edges of adjoining
bricks). Lay the second course
with the frog face downwards.

Wall
Top course of the wall forms the edging

Plate compacter
A safe, easy-to-use machine

3 While you are waiting for the mortar to set, dig out the central area within the wall to a depth of 6" (15cm). Spread a layer of hardcore and using the sledgehammer, break and compact it to a depth of 3" (75mm). Spread a thick layer of ballast and compact it with the plate compacter until 2" (50mm) deep, followed by a layer of sand compacted to a depth of 1½" (30mm). Prepare a 9' 10" (3m)-long screed board by cutting a 2¼" (65mm) (brick height) x 4½" (11.5cm) notch out of both ends. Ask someone to hold the other end and scrape off excess sand by dragging the board across the patio area while the notched ends are running against the brick wall.

Bricks
Arrange bricks (frog face down) for best fit and color effect

4 Fill low areas with more sand and compact again. Screed once more and then rake ½" (13mm) of loose sand over the whole area. Lay the bricks in a herringbone pattern. Using the brick chisel and club hammer, cut bricks to fill the small gaps. Sweep sand into the joints. Fix a pad (or piece of carpet) to the plate compacter and run the machine over the bricks.

Helpful Hint
Aim for even gaps between the bricks; stand back every now and then to check your progress. For areas larger than 10' (3m) square, use a mason's string line as a guide to laying the bricks in a straight line.

CLASSIC BIRDBATH

A birdbath must surely be one of the most decorative and interesting things to have in a garden. If you enjoy watching birds splashing the hours away, try building this straightforward pillar, which is topped with a readymade birdbath. Site it so that it can be viewed from a patio, or the house, for year-round entertainment value.

TIME
Half a day to make the foundation and four days to build the pillar.

Special Tips

This structure can also be used for mounting a sundial.

YOU WILL NEED
For a pillar 3' 7" (1.09m) high and 21¾" (55.3cm) square

Materials
- Bricks: 82
- Tiles: 36 tiles, 5½" (14.3cm) square and ⁵⁄₁₆" (8mm) thick
- Paving slab: 17¼" (44cm) square and 1⅜" (35mm) thick
- Hardcore: 3.5 cu. feet (0.1 cu. meters)
- Mortar: 1 part (26 lbs., or 12kg) cement and 4 parts (105 lbs., or 48kg) sand
- Concrete: 1 part (88 lbs., or 40kg) cement and
- 4 parts (350 lbs., or 160kg) ballast
- Wood for formwork: 4 pieces, 27" (69cm) long, 5" (12cm) wide and 2" (40mm) thick
- Wood for collar: 4 pieces, 15½" (39.3cm) long, 3" (75mm) wide and 2" (47mm) thick
- Nails: 16 x 3" (80mm)
- Birdbath dish: 13½" (34.5cm) square and 3¼" (84mm) high

Tools
- Tape measure and piece of chalk
- General-purpose saw
- Claw hammer
- Spade
- Wheelbarrow and bucket
- Sledgehammer
- Level
- Shovel and mixing board, or cement mixer
- Bricklayer's trowel and pointing trowel
- Brick chisel
- Rubber mallet
- Tile cutter

Exploded View of the Classic Birdbath

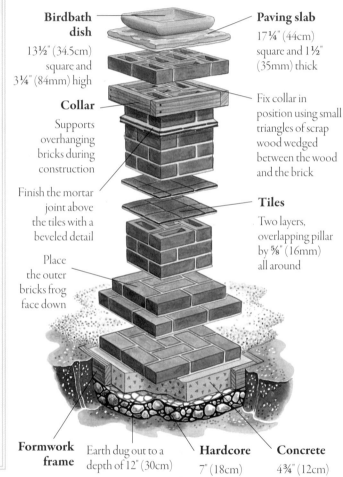

Birdbath dish
13½" (34.5cm) square and 3¼" (84mm) high

Paving slab
17¼" (44cm) square and 1½" (35mm) thick

Collar
Supports overhanging bricks during construction

Fix collar in position using small triangles of scrap wood wedged between the wood and the brick

Finish the mortar joint above the tiles with a beveled detail

Tiles
Two layers, overlapping pillar by ⅝" (16mm) all around

Place the outer bricks frog face down

Formwork frame

Earth dug out to a depth of 12" (30cm)

Hardcore
7" (18cm)

Concrete
4¾" (12cm)

A FASCINATING VIEW

Most of us enjoy watching birds in the garden, and a birdbath will help to attract them. This restrained, architectural-looking design also has other possibilities. Without the birdbath on top, the pillar can make a dramatic plinth for a classical statuette. (Fix the statue to the top with a 12" (30cm)-long steel rod ⅜" (10mm) in diameter. Drill a hole in the top of the pillar (⅜" (10mm) in diameter) with a masonry bit, making it at least 6" (15cm)

deep. Drill a 6" (15cm)-deep hole in the statue. Drop the rod into the pillar and put the statue on top. The rod will stop the statue being blown off or knocked off.) The pillar could also form the base for a sundial.

Personalize the design by choosing a birdbath handmade from metal, stone or wood, or a decorative shallow ceramic pot. The tile details could also be altered—perhaps a line of tiles on every course, or thick black slate substituted instead. Decorative patterned tiles could also be inserted into the brickwork.

Edging bricks

Place these bricks with the frog face downwards

Center bricks

Arrange the inner bricks with frog face upwards

1 Make the formwork frame using two 3" (80mm) nails at each corner. Lay the frame on the ground and roughly mark around it with the spade. Put the frame aside and dig out the marked earth to a depth of 12" (30cm). Fill the area with hardcore and compact it to a thickness of 7" (18cm) with the sledgehammer. Lay the frame on top and make sure that it is level, then fill with concrete. When the concrete is dry, practice laying the first course of bricks.

Rubber mallet

Using this avoids damaging the bricks

Level

Make sure all the bricks are bedded to the same level. Note that the outer bricks are used frog face down

Third course

Bricks placed frog face down

Pointing

Use the pointing trowel to point the joints

Joints

Note the staggered arrangement of the vertical joints

2 Chalk around the bricks. Remove them and spread mortar within the marks. Lay the first course and ensure that it is level and square by checking the side and diagonal measurements (see page 34). Lay the second course in the same way, but with the vertical joints staggered.

3 Clean up the joints of the first two courses. Practice laying the third course, which is stepped inwards. Mark its position with chalk, and lay the bricks on a bed of mortar. Repeat for the fourth course. Continue building up to the level of the tiles and leave the pillar overnight.

Leveling
Sandwich and bed the tiles in mortar and tap level

Tiles
Cut and fit the tiles so that they overhang by ⅝" (16mm)

Mortar
Rake out a little of the mortar between the tiles

4 Cut and fit two layers of tile to cover the area, allowing an overlap of ⅝" (16mm) all around the pillar. Make sure that none of the joints coincide. The tiles can be tricky to lay neatly, so work slowly and carefully. Use the level to check that they are level.

Wooden collar
Make a frame that fits loosely around the top of the pillar and wedge it in place with small triangles of scrap wood so that it cannot move. The collar will support the weight of the overhanging bricks. (When the project is complete, wait 48 hours before removing the collar)

5 Continue building up the courses of brick and tile that create the pillar, checking that each course is level and the corners remain vertical. Make the wooden collar to support the final overhanging layer of bricks and wedge it in place. Build the final course of bricks. Position the slab and clean up the joints. Place the birdbath dish on top.

> *Helpful Hint*
> Positioning the collar is difficult to do on your own, so ask somebody to help. If the collar keeps slipping down or going crooked, try using differently shaped wedges, and more of them.

PLANTED PATIO

Just imagine a warm summer's evening, when you can sit outside enjoying the stored heat given off by the patio, and wafts of scent from surrounding plants. This patio design incorporates beds of earth, which have been planted with a selection of herbs. Concrete paving blocks, bricks or clay paving blocks can be used for the paving.

TIME
Five days to prepare the foundation and two days to lay the blocks.

Special Tips
If you want a different pattern of blocks, experiment by arranging them on the ground.

YOU WILL NEED
For a planted patio 15' 9" (4.81m) square

 Materials

- Concrete paving blocks: 714 blocks, 8" (20cm) long, 4" (100mm) wide and 2" (50mm) thick (or bricks or clay paving blocks—if using these, adjust quantity, overall patio measurements and depth of foundation)
- Hardcore: 88 cu. feet (2.5 cu. meters)
- Nails: 172 x 1½" (38mm)
- Concrete: 1 part (1,100 lbs., or 500kg) cement and 4 parts (2 tons) ballast

- Mortar: 1 part (165 lbs., or 75kg) cement and 4 parts (660 lbs., or 300kg) sand
- Wood for formwork: 92' (28m) of 1" x 6" (22mm x 15cm) section
- Wood for formwork stakes: 56 pieces, 12" (30cm) long, 2" (35mm) wide and 1" (22mm) thick
- Wood for tamping board: 1 piece, 5' 3" (1.6m) long, 4" (100mm) wide and 1" (22mm) thick

Tools

- Tape measure, stakes and string
- Spade and fork
- Wheelbarrow and bucket
- General-purpose saw
- Claw hammer
- Level

- Club hammer
- Sledgehammer
- Shovel and mixing board, or cement mixer
- Brick chisel
- Pointing trowel
- Gardener's trowel

SETTING THE STYLE

This design offers a blend of planting and paving reminiscent of a medieval herb garden. It can be enjoyed as a pathway through a miniature landscape, or somewhere to sit in peace on your own, or as a place to savor the fragrance of herbs. If you wish, you can change the balance of planting to paving, or move the planting to one side and have a larger paved area for sitting.

Patios require a big investment in time and materials, so make sure that you can manage a project of this size. You shouldn't come across any pipes while digging the foundation, because it isn't very deep, but always be cautious and get advice if you uncover pipes that you were not expecting. The major part of the work is the digging and the setting out of the wooden formwork, so don't be dismayed if things seem slow at first.

Cut-Away View of the Planted Patio

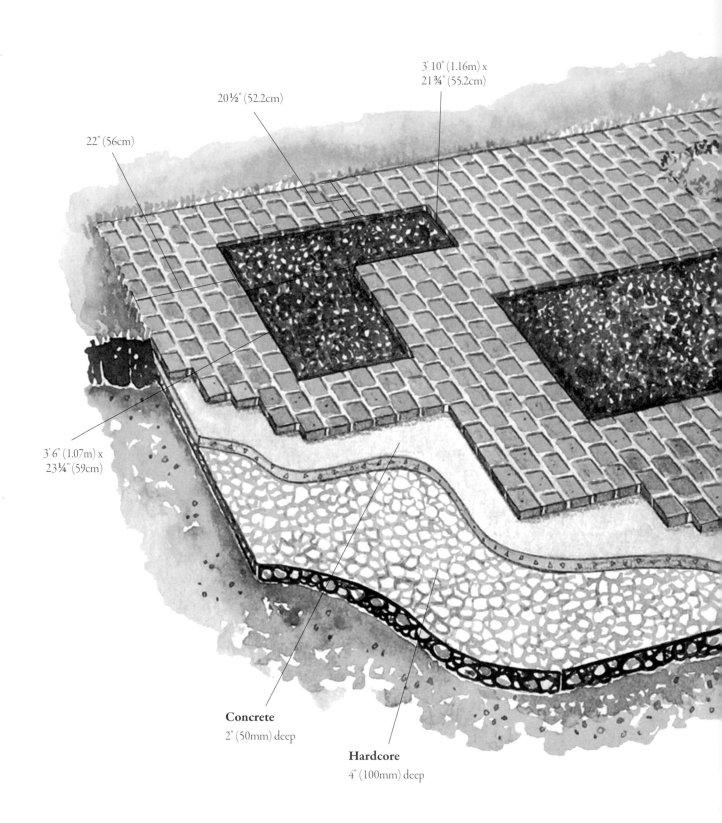

3' 10" (1.16m) x
21¾" (55.2cm)

20½" (52.2cm)

22" (56cm)

3' 6" (1.07m) x
23¼" (59cm)

Concrete
2" (50mm) deep

Hardcore
4" (100mm) deep

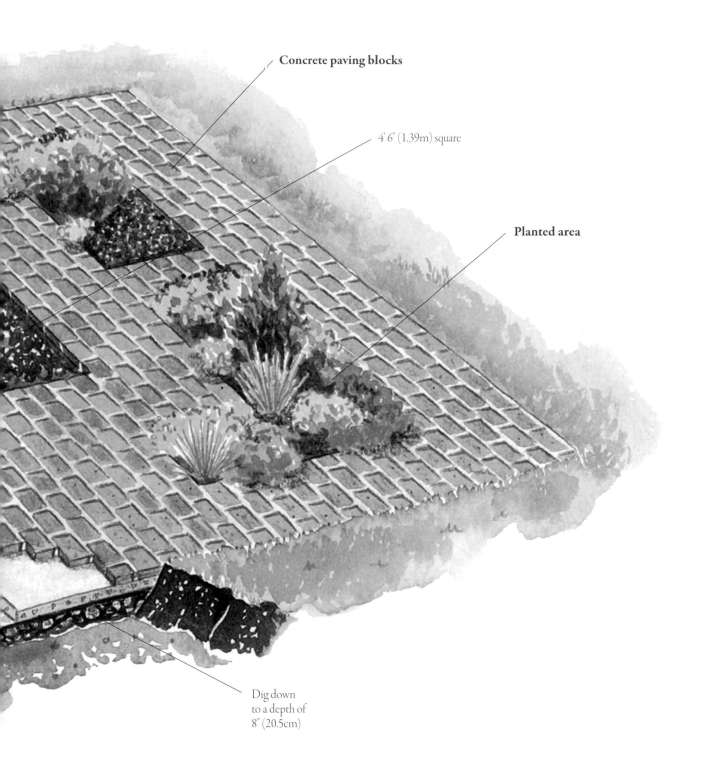

Concrete paving blocks

4' 6" (1.39m) square

Planted area

Dig down
to a depth of
8" (20.5cm)

Hardcore

Compact to a depth of 4" (100mm) and 1⅛"–1⅝" (30–40mm) lower than the formwork

Formwork

Build formwork frames using two nails at each corner. Nail stakes to the inside of the frames

1 Dig out a level area of earth 15' 9" (4.81m) square and 8" (20.5cm) deep. Mark out the paved and planted areas with stakes and string. Make up formwork frames to the size and shape of the planting areas. Knock these into the ground so that they are level with each other. Spread hardcore where the paving will be, and compact it to a depth of 4" (100mm).

> ## Helpful Hint
> You will get a slightly better result if you can leave a gap between the hardcore and the formwork. With this method, the concrete will form a stronger edge around the planting areas.

Concrete

Should have a crumbly texture

2 Mix up some concrete using very little water (it should be crumbly), and shovel it over the hardcore. Use the tamping board to tamp the concrete level with the top of the formwork. It is possible to work on your own, but the task is much easier if you have help. Either way, do not step on the concrete, and do not try to build more than a quarter of the patio at one time.

Tamping

Tamp the concrete level with the top of the formwork

Bedding
Dampen the underside of the bricks and wiggle into place

String line
Use a taut mason's string line as a guide

Joints
Aim for joints that are about ½" (15mm) wide

3 Without waiting for the concrete to dry, set up a mason's string line to indicate where to lay the first line of blocks and gently bed each block, leaving gaps of about ½" (15mm) between them. The concrete is already level, so there is no need to tap the blocks down or check levels—just wiggle them into position and occasionally stand back to check that your lines are straight and gaps are equal.

Mortar
Push crumbly mortar into the joints

Pointing
Use the handle of the pointing trowel to smooth and finish the joints

Formwork
Remove the formwork and fill with earth

Plants
Choose plants carefully. Before planting, lay them out in their pots to look at the pattern you are creating. Take into account their size when fully grown

Earth
Use a planting mixture to suit your plants

4 Use a brick chisel and club hammer to cut blocks to fill in small spaces. Mix up some mortar using very little water (like the concrete, it should be crumbly) and scrape this into the gaps. Push it down into the gaps until you have filled the full depth. Finish the joints.

5 Leave the concrete and mortar to set fully (or wait at least two days) and then clean up any excess mortar. Remove the formwork, loosen the earth in the planting areas with the fork, and top them up with good soil or compost to the level of the bricks.

DECORATIVE RAISED BED

Raised beds are a good idea: not only do they give you the chance to increase the planting area in your garden, but better still—especially if you find it difficult to bend—they bring the garden up to a more manageable height and make it very easy to tend the plants. A raised bed can make a very suitable home for rock garden plants, enabling you to enjoy these miniature plants at close quarters.

 TIME

One weekend (longer if you need to build a foundation).

Special Tips

You may need to use an angle grinder, which requires safety precautions (see pages 24 and 43).

YOU WILL NEED

For a raised bed 3' 9" x 3' 9" (1.15 x 1.15m) minus square section to create L-shape, and 22" (56cm) high

 Materials

- Bricks: 128
- Decorative tiles: 2 tiles, 8½" (21.5cm) square and 1⅛" (28mm) thick
- Coping tiles: 14 tiles, 11½" (29cm) long,

5¼" (13.2cm) wide and 1" (26mm) thick
- Mortar: 1 part (33 lbs., or 15kg) cement and 4 parts (130 lbs., or 60kg) sand

Tools

- Tape measure, straightedge about 4' (1.2m) long, and a piece of chalk
- Shovel and mixing board, or cement mixer
- Bricklayer's trowel and pointing trowel

- Level
- Bricklayer's hammer
- Brick chisel
- Club hammer
- Angle grinder (may be required to cut the coping tiles)

RAISING THE STANDARDS

As with most projects, there are options and variations you might prefer instead of building exactly to the given specifications. If you are thinking about altering the size, remember that the size and shape of the bed both need careful consideration—it is tempting to build a bigger structure, but there is a danger of creating something that requires a massive amount of earth. This narrow corner design is great for small plants and doesn't need tons of soil to fill it. The decorative tiles make the building procedure more complicated, but are worth the extra trouble.

If you want to change the appearance of the raised bed, don't settle for boring materials until you have scoured the salvage yards for great-looking terracotta details or old-style patterned tiles. Brightly colored Victorian glazed tiles with floral designs will look wonderful set against the warm colors of the brick. You may also want to consider using contrasting colors of brick in lines or patterns, as used in the Storage Seat project on page 94.

Cross-Section of the Decorative Raised Bed

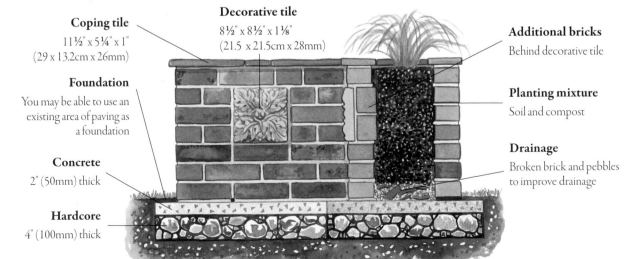

Coping tile
11½" x 5¼" x 1"
(29 x 13.2cm x 26mm)

Decorative tile
8½" x 8½" x 1⅛"
(21.5 x 21.5cm x 28mm)

Additional bricks
Behind decorative tile

Foundation
You may be able to use an existing area of paving as a foundation

Planting mixture
Soil and compost

Concrete
2" (50mm) thick

Drainage
Broken brick and pebbles to improve drainage

Hardcore
4" (100mm) thick

Plan View Showing the First Course of Bricks

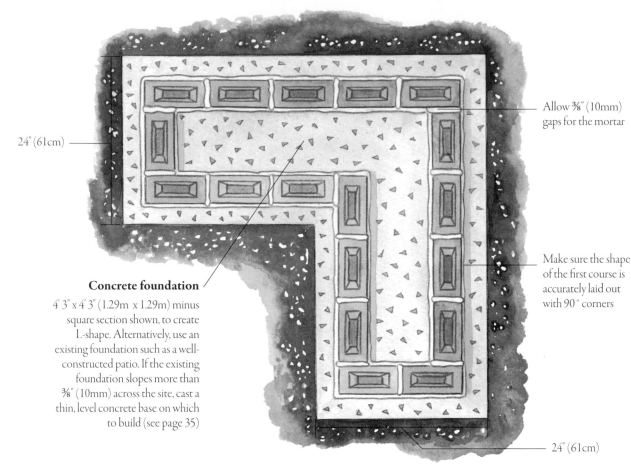

Allow ⅜" (10mm) gaps for the mortar

24" (61cm)

Make sure the shape of the first course is accurately laid out with 90° corners

Concrete foundation

4' 3" x 4' 3" (1.29m x 1.29m) minus square section shown, to create L-shape. Alternatively, use an existing foundation such as a well-constructed patio. If the existing foundation slopes more than ⅜" (10mm) across the site, cast a thin, level concrete base on which to build (see page 35)

24" (61cm)

Detail Showing the Recess for the Decorative Tile

Incorporate a 9¼" (23.5cm)-square recess in the wall to take a decorative tile

Cut bricks neatly and arrange them so that only the best edges are on view (with a half-brick, the cut end can face inward)

Two bricks laid behind the decorative tile complete the wall (place the tile first)

Exploded View of the Decorative Raised Bed

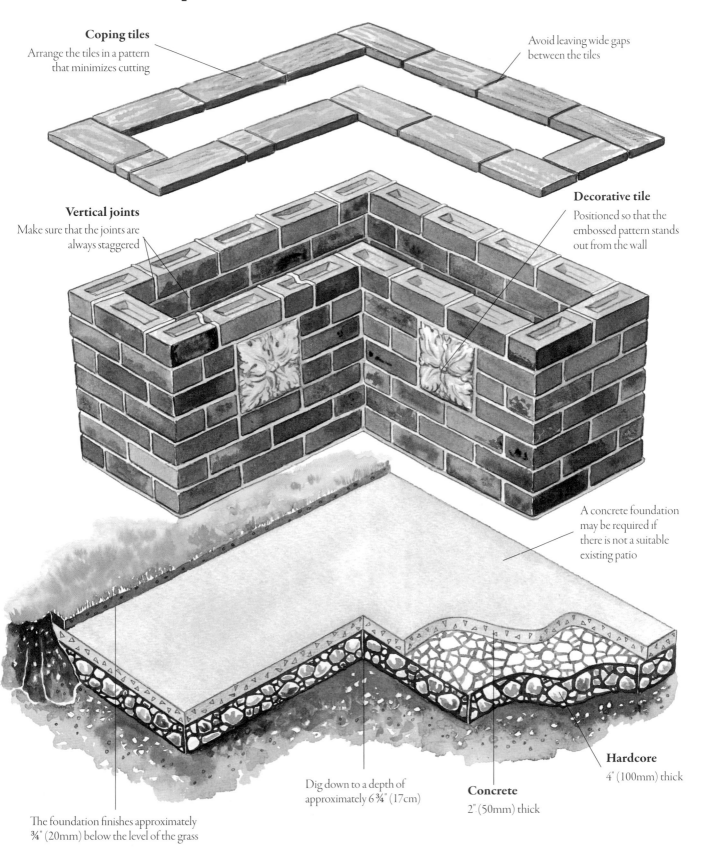

Coping tiles
Arrange the tiles in a pattern that minimizes cutting

Avoid leaving wide gaps between the tiles

Vertical joints
Make sure that the joints are always staggered

Decorative tile
Positioned so that the embossed pattern stands out from the wall

A concrete foundation may be required if there is not a suitable existing patio

The foundation finishes approximately ¾" (20mm) below the level of the grass

Dig down to a depth of approximately 6¾" (17cm)

Concrete
2" (50mm) thick

Hardcore
4" (100mm) thick

STEP-BY-STEP: MAKING THE DECORATIVE RAISED BED

First course
Arrange the bricks in the correct position, leaving ⅜" (10mm) gaps in between

Marking out
Use a piece of chalk and a straightedge to mark out the shape

Corners
Check that the bricks form 90° corners

Leveling
Use the level to help position the bricks accurately

Straight sides
Check that the bricks are in straight lines using the edge of the level

1 Work out where you would like the bed. We have put it on the corner of a patio that has a foundation sufficiently adequate to support the additional weight of a raised bed. See pages 32–35 if you need to build a foundation. Practice arranging the first course of bricks to establish the size and shape of the bed, and use the tape measure, chalk and straightedge to mark around them.

2 Lay the first course of bricks on a bed of mortar. Use the level to check that the bricks are accurately placed and stand back to scrutinize your work. The overall shape should have 90° corners, the sides should be straight, and the gaps between the bricks should be equal.

3 Lay a further two courses, making sure that each one is level and the vertical joints occur in the correct staggered positions. Clean up the joints using the pointing trowel.

Pointing
Use the pointing trowel to scrape away the excess mortar and smooth the joints between the bricks

Joints inside wall
Don't worry too much about the appearance of the mortar joints inside the structure—just scrape out the excess

Bricks

Use two bricks to weigh down the piece of wood that holds the tile in place

Decorative tile

Check that it is positioned centrally and vertically within the space, and that the pattern stands out from the bricks

4 Build the next three courses, leaving square spaces in the front-facing walls to receive the decorative tiles. Spread mortar in these spaces and position the tiles. Hold each tile in position by placing a piece of wood across the top of the walls and weighting it with a couple of bricks. Put bricks behind the tile to support it (see hint).

Level

Use the edge of the level to help you position the coping tiles in a straight line

5 Complete the last course of bricks. Note how the bricks in this course are cut (using the bricklayer's hammer) and arranged so that the joints do not coincide with the edges of the tile below (see main picture). Practice arranging the coping tiles in a pattern that minimizes cutting. Use the brick chisel and club hammer, or angle grinder, to cut tiles. Bed the coping tiles on ⅜" (10mm) of mortar, using the side of the level to help align the edges of the tiles.

SIMPLE GARDEN WALL

There is something very enjoyable about building a simple brick wall—the process of troweling slices of soft, smooth mortar, and placing one brick upon another, is a great escape from everyday worries. This freestanding low wall is suitable for a front garden wall, a wall around a raised patio, or a retaining wall for a small flower border. Or perhaps you have an unstable wall with missing bricks, which needs replacing.

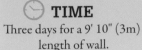 **TIME**

Three days for a 9' 10" (3m) length of wall.

Special Tips

If you want a bigger wall, see page 50 for details on wall size and safety.

YOU WILL NEED

For a wall 9' 10" (3m) long and 20½" (51.8cm) high

 Materials

- Bricks: 180
- Tiles: 36 tiles, 10½" (26.5cm) long, 7" (17.5cm) wide and ⅜" (10mm) thick
- Mortar: 1 part (55 lbs., or 25kg) cement and 4 parts (220 lbs., or 100kg) sand
- Wood for leveling board: 1 piece, 9' 10" (3m) long, 4" (100mm) wide and 1" (22mm) thick

Tools

- Shovel and mixing board, or cement mixer
- Wheelbarrow and bucket
- Bricklayer's trowel and pointing trowel
- Level
- Bricklayer's hammer

THE GREAT DIVIDE

A two-brick-thick wall is a good choice for most garden walls and will look better and last longer than the single-brick alternative. The pattern of bricks used in this wall is a traditional arrangement, and the layers of protruding tiles and beveled mortar detail are not just for decoration—to some extent they also protect the structure from water erosion. If you are contemplating a higher wall, you will need extra support (see page 50 on supporting piers and buttresses) and you would certainly need a more substantial foundation. For a wall that is twice as high, increase the size of the concrete foundation slab to three times the width of the wall, and increase the thickness of the slab by 1⅛" (30mm). A beginner should not attempt to build a wall higher than about 6' 6" (2m).

This low wall is built on an existing foundation (see page 35 for how to assess suitability). See page 50 for how to build curved walls, change angles and build around corners.

Cross-Section Detail of the Simple Garden Wall

Coping bricks

Bricks
Laid in normal running bond

Concrete
3½" (90mm) thick

Hardcore
3½" (90mm) thick

Tiles
Two layers of decorative tiles help the wall shed rainwater

Soldier bricks
Headers (ends) facing forwards

You may be able to use an existing foundation such as a strongly built patio

Cut-Away Detail of the Simple Garden Wall

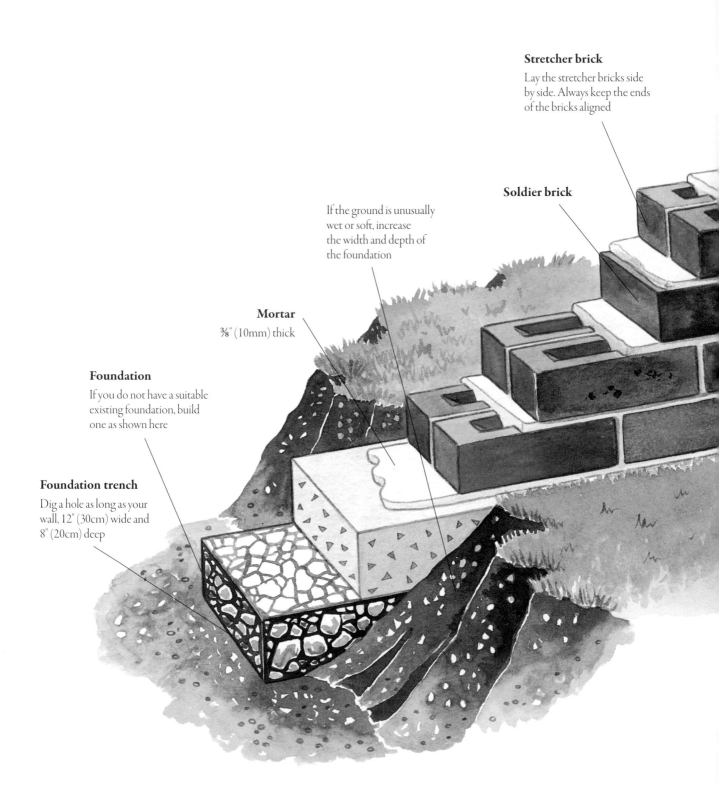

Stretcher brick
Lay the stretcher bricks side by side. Always keep the ends of the bricks aligned

Soldier brick

If the ground is unusually wet or soft, increase the width and depth of the foundation

Mortar
⅜" (10mm) thick

Foundation
If you do not have a suitable existing foundation, build one as shown here

Foundation trench
Dig a hole as long as your wall, 12" (30cm) wide and 8" (20cm) deep

Tile
Arrange the tiles
so that the joints
are staggered

Coping brick

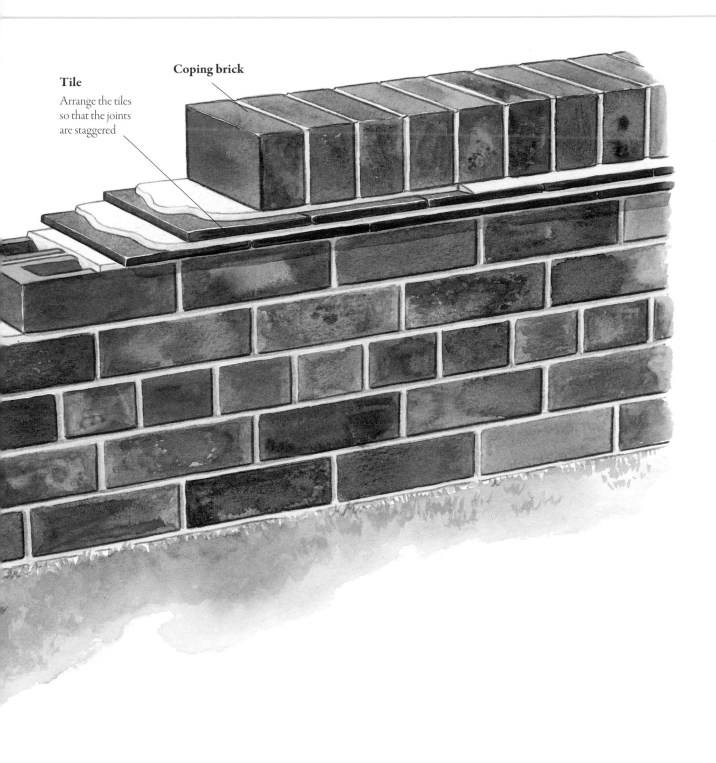

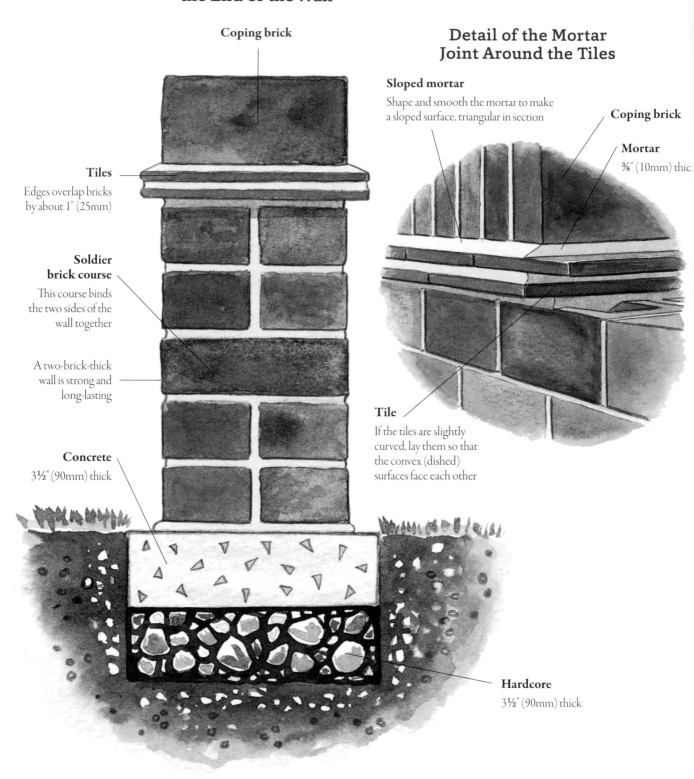

Cross-Section Detail of the End of the Wall

Coping brick

Detail of the Mortar Joint Around the Tiles

Sloped mortar
Shape and smooth the mortar to make a sloped surface, triangular in section

Coping brick

Mortar
⅜" (10mm) thic[k]

Tiles
Edges overlap bricks by about 1" (25mm)

Soldier brick course
This course binds the two sides of the wall together

A two-brick-thick wall is strong and long-lasting

Tile
If the tiles are slightly curved, lay them so that the convex (dished) surfaces face each other

Concrete
3½" (90mm) thick

Hardcore
3½" (90mm) thick

1 If there is a suitable foundation (see page 35), you can start laying the bricks. Lay the first course of bricks on a generous bed of mortar. The bricks in each row should be equally spaced (⅜" (10mm) joints) and placed exactly opposite each other. Check that the bricks are level and make adjustments as necessary.

First course
Bed pairs of bricks on mortar

Foundation
In this instance, there is a good, solid foundation under the patio

2 Continue building the wall, this time staggering the joints of the second course so that they occur halfway along the bricks of the first course. Check that the course is horizontal using the leveling board and the level. (At this point, you could also use a line set to help you, which establishes a level and a straight line, and is usually employed in the construction of long walls and houses—see page 20.)

Leveling
Use the leveling board and level

Cleaning up
Wait until the mortar has partly dried, then clean it up

Bond
Build two courses of running bond

Aligning

Use the handle of the hammer to tap the bricks into line

Third course

Lay the soldier brick course, with every other brick centered on the vertical joints in the course underneath

3 The third course is of soldier bricks, with the headers (ends) of the bricks facing forwards. In this course, alternate bricks should be centered on a joint underneath. Use the level to check that the wall is vertical, and make any necessary corrections by gently tapping bricks into line using the handle of the bricklayer's hammer. Build the fourth and fifth courses as for the first and second courses.

Tile position

Arrange the tiles so that there is an equal overhang at each side

Tile joints

Sandwich the tiles so that the joints are staggered

4 Lay the tiles on a ⅜" (10mm)-thick bed of mortar, and avoid leaving any gaps in between them. Complete the first layer and proceed to the next. Start the second layer with half a tile (break with the bricklayer's hammer) so that the joints between the rows of tiles are staggered.

Helpful Hint

The shape and texture of the tiles will affect the appearance of the wall. Do not use concrete tiles (the edges are not decorative) or tiles that are very curved or smooth—both can be troublesome to work with.

Coping bricks
Bedded on their
stretcher face

Frogs
Should all
face in the
same direction

5 Spread mortar along the top
of the wall and lay the coping
bricks on their stretcher face
(side), with all the frogs facing in
the same direction. Finish with
the frog of the last brick facing
inwards (so that the frog is not
visible). Check that the coping is
straight and level.

Pointing
Point the top
joints so that
they are smooth
and flush

Protection
The idea of the
coping bricks
and tiles is that
they make rain
run off without
touching the wall

Mortar
Angle the
mortar down
to the edge of
the tiles

6 Clean up all the joints that
still need doing and then
concentrate on the mortar detail
above the line of tiles. Spread
mortar along the join and smooth
it to form a sloped surface that
is triangular in section (see
drawing).

STORAGE SEAT

If your shed is bulging at the seams, this useful storage seat will provide a practical and attractive solution. It also gives you the opportunity to build a decorative brick box in the English diaper tradition (an all-over surface decoration of a small repeated pattern such as diamonds or squares, using colored, projecting or recessed bricks).

⏱ TIME
Three days if using an existing foundation.

Special Tips

The seat is heavy. You may want to consider a hinged design.

YOU WILL NEED

For a storage seat 4' 8" (1.43m) long, 26" (66.2cm) wide and 20¼" (51.3cm) high

Materials
- Bricks: 67 light-colored bricks and 23 dark-colored bricks
- Mortar: 1 part (22 lbs., or 10kg) cement and 4 parts (88 lbs., or 40kg) sand
- Wood for seat frame: 2 pieces, 4' 8" (1.43m) long, 3" (63mm) wide and 2" (38mm) thick; and 6 pieces, 23" (58.6cm) long, 3" (63mm) wide and 2" (38mm) thick

- Wood for seat planks: 6 pieces, 4' 8" (1.43m) long, 4" (100mm) wide and 1" (20mm) thick
- Plywood (exterior grade): 1 piece, 4' 8" (1.43m) long, 26" (66.2cm) wide and ¼" (5mm) thick (under-seat board)
- Nails: 16 x 4" (100mm) (frame) and 36 x 2" (50mm) (seat planks)

Tools
- Tape measure and a piece of chalk
- Level
- Shovel and mixing board, or cement mixer
- Wheelbarrow and bucket

- Bricklayer's trowel and pointing trowel
- Bricklayer's hammer
- General-purpose saw
- Claw hammer

ON THE BENCH

Have you ever looked at a plastic storage chest and thought that it would be really useful for the garden, but decided that it was far too ugly? Well, if you like good-looking, hard-working garden structures, this project might appeal to you. We have built the storage seat on the edge of a patio, where it can be used to hide away tools, pots and other paraphernalia, keeping them protected from the weather. The slatted seat is made from preserved pine, with an under-seat board of exterior plywood beneath the slats to stop rain getting into the storage space. Oak slats would look even better, but are more expensive. If you don't need storage space and just want a seat, you could make a lower structure and fashion the seat out of chunky railroad ties. The diamond pattern of dark bricks is not difficult to achieve and can be altered if you want a different effect. Bands of different-colored bricks, contrasting corner bricks, terracotta tiles and glazed tiles are some of the options open to you.

Front View of the Storage Seat

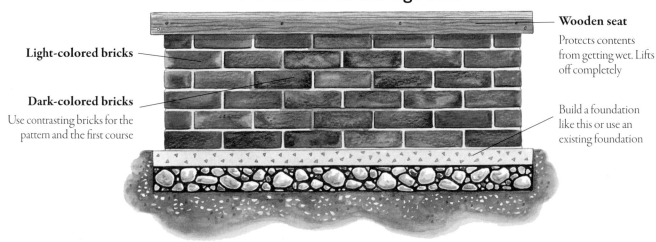

Light-colored bricks

Dark-colored bricks
Use contrasting bricks for the pattern and the first course

Wooden seat
Protects contents from getting wet. Lifts off completely

Build a foundation like this or use an existing foundation

Exploded View of the Storage Seat

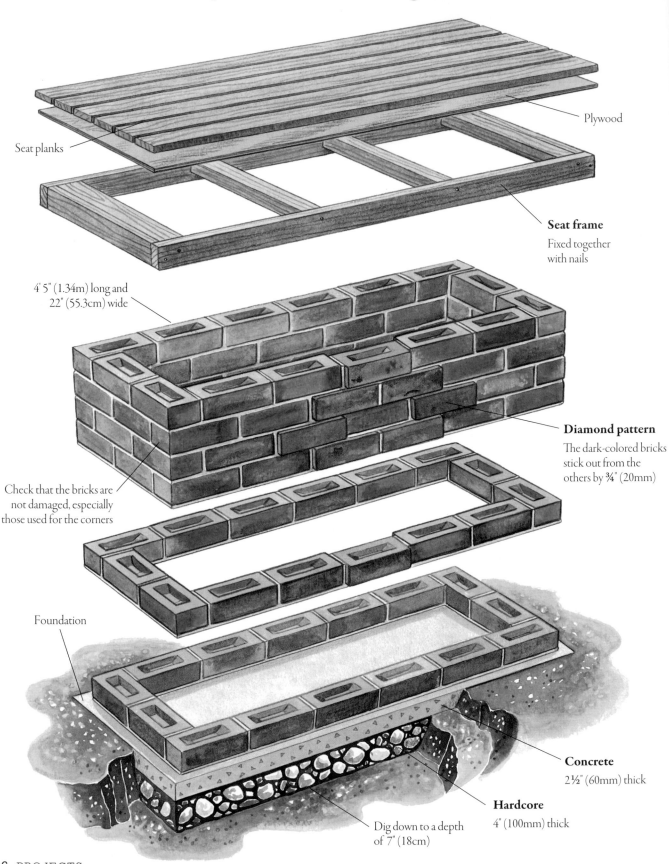

Plywood

Seat planks

Seat frame
Fixed together
with nails

4' 5" (1.34m) long and
22" (55.3cm) wide

Diamond pattern
The dark-colored bricks
stick out from the
others by ¾" (20mm)

Check that the bricks are
not damaged, especially
those used for the corners

Foundation

Concrete
2½" (60mm) thick

Hardcore
4" (100mm) thick

Dig down to a depth
of 7" (18cm)

Plan View Showing the First Course of Bricks

Concrete foundation
4' 8" x 24" (1.43m x 61.8cm)

First course
4' 5" x 22" (1.34m x 55.3cm)

Use dark-colored bricks for
the first course

The first brick of the diamond
pattern (second course)

Cut-Away View Showing the Wood Seat

Seat planks
6 pieces, 4' 8" (1.43m) long, 4" (100mm)
wide and 1" (20mm) thick

Nails
2" (50mm) long

Seat frame is fixed together
with 4" (100mm) nails

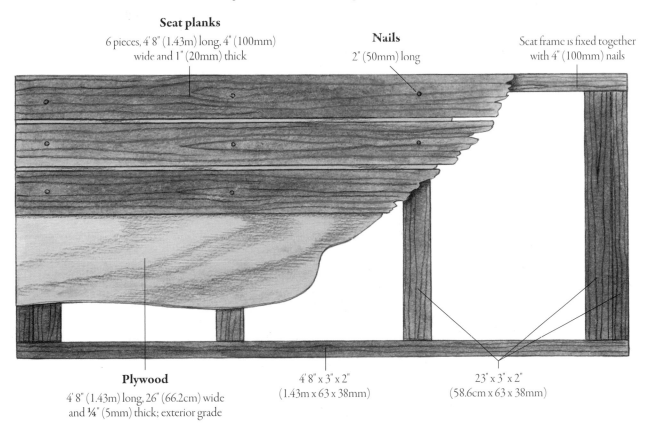

Plywood
4' 8" (1.43m) long, 26" (66.2cm) wide
and ¼" (5mm) thick; exterior grade

4' 8" x 3" x 2"
(1.43m x 63 x 38mm)

23" x 3" x 2"
(58.6cm x 63 x 38mm)

Level

Make sure that the first course is level

First course

Bed the bricks on a generous layer of mortar

1 Chalk out an area, 4' 5" (1.34m) long and 22" (55.3cm) wide, on the foundation using the tape measure and a piece of wood for the seat frame. (See page 35 if using an existing foundation.) Lay the first course of dark bricks. Make sure that it is level, straight, and the joints are all ⅜" (10mm) wide.

Helpful Hint

If you change the size of the structure, try and keep to using whole bricks. If it is to be built against a wall, build it in the same way—don't be tempted to build just three sides, as it will make the structure very weak.

Second course

Arrange the second course so that it is staggered with the first

Hammer

Use the handle to nudge and adjust the bricks

2 Continue laying the bricks, using the light-colored bricks for the rest of the courses and the remaining dark bricks for the diamond pattern. The diamond bricks stick out from the others by ¾" (20mm). Stagger the joints in each course.

Mortar
Before removing excess mortar, wait until it has partly dried

Level
Check the alignment of the bricks

Diaper bricks
The dark bricks forming the pattern need to project by ¾" (20mm)

3 While building the courses, keep checking that the bricks are correctly positioned in a straight line, with equal gaps between them. Take extra care over the bricks used for the pattern, because any mistakes will be obvious. Use the level to check the vertical alignment of the joints within the pattern.

Bricklayer's trowel
Use this as a work surface while you fill gaps with the pointing trowel

Pointing
Slide slices of mortar into the joints

Seat planks
Nail them through the seat board and into the frame

Nails
Use two short nails at each end of the planks and one every so often along the length

Seat board
Plywood sandwiched between the planks and the frame

4 Clean up all the joints, taking extra care on the front face of the structure and around the diamond pattern. Fill in any gaps, using the pointing trowel to slice slivers of mortar off a dollop of mortar held on the bricklayer's trowel, and force them into the cavity.

5 Build the seat to fit around the top of the wall (don't forget that the top brick of the diamond pattern sticks out by ¾" (20mm)). Assemble the seat frame using the long nails, lay the seat board on top of it, and cover it with equally spaced seat planks. Attach with the short nails.

GATEWAY COLUMNS

Get rid of decrepit, leaning wooden fence posts, or ugly concrete blocks, and build a noble gateway in the great country house tradition—a bold and dashing piece of garden architecture, which will make a splendid grand entrance to add class to your driveway or front path, or to any part of the garden. The distinctive ball finials magically transform straightforward columns into something special.

⏱ **TIME**

One day to prepare the foundation and three days to complete the columns.

Special Tips

If you build columns higher than these, you must also increase their width and depth.

YOU WILL NEED

For gateway columns 3' 9" (1.15m) high and 2' 9" (83.2cm) apart

Materials

- Bricks: 172
- Tiles: 16 tiles, 8⅝" (22cm) long, 6" (15.5cm) wide and ⅜" (10mm) thick
- Stone or concrete balls: 2, each 11" (28cm) high, with a base 10⅝" (27cm) square
- Hardcore: 10 cu. feet (0.3 cu. meters)
- Concrete: 1 part (265 lbs., or 120kg) cement and 4 parts (1,050 lbs., or 480kg) ballast
- Mortar: 1 part (44 lbs., or 20kg) cement and 4 parts (175 lbs., or 80kg) sand

Tools

- Tape measure, stakes, string, straightedge and a piece of chalk
- Level
- Spade and fork
- Wheelbarrow and bucket
- Shovel and mixing board, or cement mixer
- Sledgehammer
- Bricklayer's trowel and pointing trowel
- Bricklayer's hammer
- Brick chisel

MAKING A GRAND ENTRANCE

Stately homes often have ornate ironwork front gates hung from huge, formal pillars topped by a striking sculpture such as a giant stone eagle. These gateway columns are not quite so imposing, but they have the same classic pedigree and, in a more restrained way, look grand. We have built them to act as a visual divider between a patio and the rest of the garden, with the columns attached to low brick walls. The columns could also be used either side of a small gate in front of your house, or to span a flight of steps in a terraced garden. They can be used as a feature anywhere in the garden—for example wherever there is a pathway leading from one distinct area of the garden to another, or where there is a change in levels, you can build columns and divide off the area by adding a brick wall, wooden picket fence or a beautiful hedge.

Perspective View of the Gateway Columns

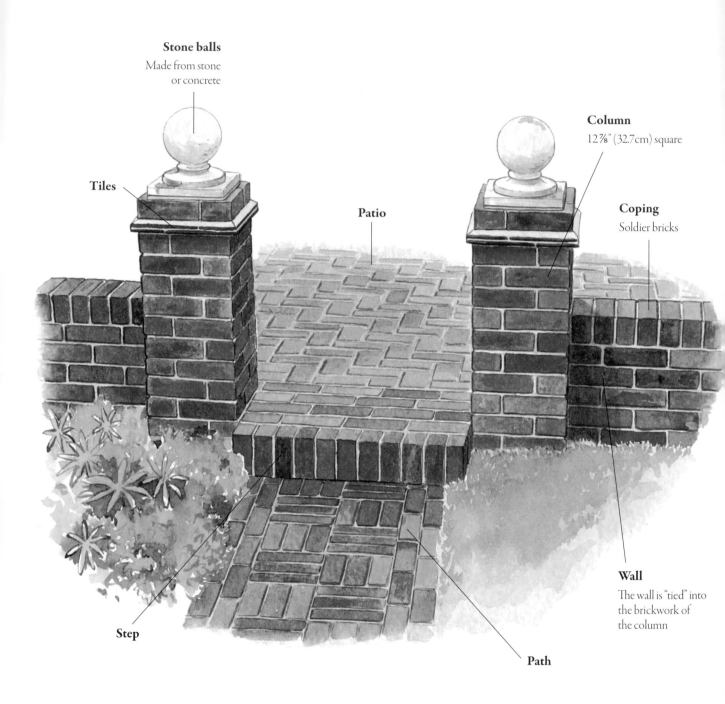

Stone balls
Made from stone
or concrete

Tiles

Patio

Column
12⅞" (32.7cm) square

Coping
Soldier bricks

Wall
The wall is "tied" into
the brickwork of
the column

Step

Path

Exploded View of the Gateway Columns

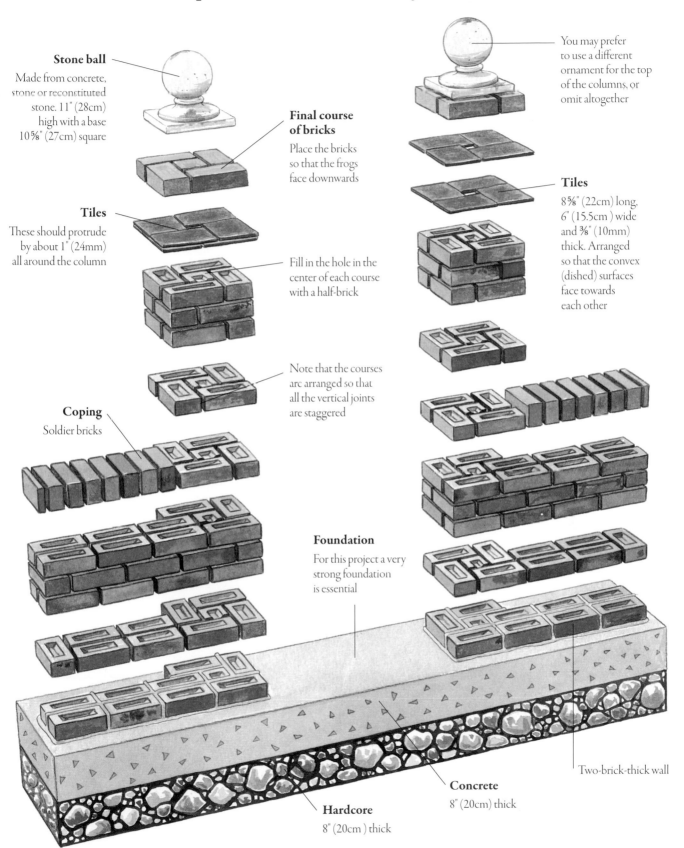

Stone ball

Made from concrete, stone or reconstituted stone. 11" (28cm) high with a base 10⅝" (27cm) square

Final course of bricks

Place the bricks so that the frogs face downwards

Tiles

These should protrude by about 1" (24mm) all around the column

Fill in the hole in the center of each course with a half-brick

Note that the courses are arranged so that all the vertical joints are staggered

Coping

Soldier bricks

Foundation

For this project a very strong foundation is essential

You may prefer to use a different ornament for the top of the columns, or omit altogether

Tiles

8⅝" (22cm) long, 6" (15.5cm) wide and ⅜" (10mm) thick. Arranged so that the convex (dished) surfaces face towards each other

Two-brick-thick wall

Concrete

8" (20cm) thick

Hardcore

8" (20cm) thick

Front View of the Gateway Columns

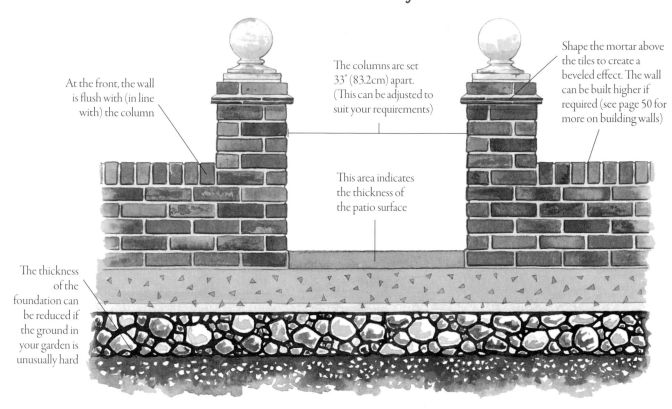

At the front, the wall is flush with (in line with) the column

The columns are set 33" (83.2cm) apart. (This can be adjusted to suit your requirements)

This area indicates the thickness of the patio surface

Shape the mortar above the tiles to create a beveled effect. The wall can be built higher if required (see page 50 for more on building walls)

The thickness of the foundation can be reduced if the ground in your garden is unusually hard

Back View of the Gateway Columns

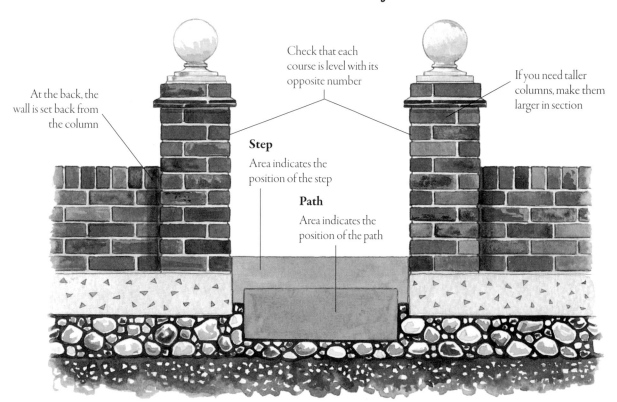

At the back, the wall is set back from the column

Check that each course is level with its opposite number

If you need taller columns, make them larger in section

Step
Area indicates the position of the step

Path
Area indicates the position of the path

Bonds
Study the working drawing carefully

Level
Check that each brick is correctly positioned before placing the next one. Ensure that the corners of the column are true

1 Plan the columns and adjoining walls. If you need steps between the columns, see page 53. Build a foundation using at least 8" (20cm) of concrete over 8" (20cm) of compacted hardcore. Mark out the first course and practice laying the bricks without mortar. Lay two courses with mortar, making checks as you go.

Helpful Hint
An inadequate foundation (too narrow, too thin or badly made) may cause a pillar to crack or lean. If in doubt, build a bigger foundation than you think is needed.

2 During construction of the columns, clean up the joints between the bricks using the tip of the pointing trowel. Try not to smear mortar on the surface of the bricks (especially wet mortar), and avoid raking out too much mortar from between the bricks.

Mortar
Ideally, excess mortar should be left alone until it is has dried to a crumbly texture

Pointing
Point the joints to a raked finish

3 Complete laying the courses of the low brick walls, and continue building the columns for another two courses. Lay a coping of soldier bricks, starting at the column end. Use the level and handle of the bricklayer's hammer to push the coping into alignment. Clean up the wall joints.

Soldier brick coping
Lay the bricks on their stretcher face

Pointing the soldier bricks
Point the coping to a smooth finish

Pointing the wall face
Fill any gaps. Rake out the mortar to create a weathered finish

Tiles
Old roof tiles are perfect for this

Arrangment
Sandwich the tiles in place so that the joints are staggered

Tile overhang
Make sure that the overhang is equal all the way around

4 Continue building the columns, all the time checking that the courses in each column are level with each other and the sides and corners of the columns are vertical. Bed two layers of tiles on mortar in the pattern shown. Note that if the tiles are curved, they should be placed so that the first layer curves upwards and the second layer curves downwards (and the joints need to be staggered).

Ball finial
Dampen the base of the finial prior to bedding it on mortar

Frogs
The bricks at the top of the column are placed with the frog facing downwards

5 Build a final course of bricks on top of the tiles, but this time turn the bricks so the frogs are facing downwards. Practice positioning the balls on top of the columns, and when you have established the correct position, draw around them with chalk. Spread a layer of mortar inside the marked area and lower the balls into place. Inspect all the brickwork for any gaps that need filling, and clean up the joints as necessary.

STRAWBERRY BARREL

How many times have you planted out your strawberries, only to find them eradicated by a slithering army of slugs? This strawberry barrel will help provide a defence by literally lifting your strawberries up to a new level, making access harder for predators. The strawberries are also easier to pick from their elevated position, and make an attractive feature draped over the brickwork.

⏱ TIME

One day to prepare the foundation and three days to complete the columns.

Special Tips

Don't be tempted to build without a trammel, because the results will be disappointing.

YOU WILL NEED

For a strawberry barrel 3' 9" (1.15m) high and 29½" (75.2cm) in diameter

 Materials

- Bricks: 117
- Slate: 12 pieces, 8¾" (22.5cm) long, 6½" (16.6cm) wide and ¼" (6mm) thick
- Pebbles: 400, ½"–¾" (15–20mm) in diameter
- Hardcore: 3½ cu. feet (0.1 cu. meters)
- Concrete: 1 part (66 lbs., or 30kg) cement and 4 parts (265 lbs., or 120kg) ballast

- Mortar: 1 part (55 lbs., or 25kg) cement and 4 parts (220 lbs., or 100kg) sand
- Wood for trammel: 1 piece, 16¼" (41.2cm) long, 3" (65mm) wide and 1" (25mm) thick
- Metal tube: 5' 6" (1.66m) long and 1" (27mm) in diameter
- Land drainage pipe: 3' 3" (1m) long, 4" (100mm) in diameter (to help water drainage in the soil)

 Tools

- Tape measure, stakes and string
- Spade
- Wheelbarrow and bucket
- Shovel and mixing board, or cement mixer
- Sledgehammer
- Bricklayer's hammer and club hammer

- Level
- Drill and bit to match diameter of the metal tube
- Locking pliers
- Brick chisel
- Bricklayer's trowel and pointing trowel
- Rubber mallet
- Tile cutter

A STRAWBERRY PASSION

This sculptural planter is specifically designed for growing strawberries and presenting them in a decorative way. It is probably best to build it in a sunny spot to one side of the garden, or as the centerpiece of a vegetable patch or decorative cottage garden. If you intend to use the structure to plant flowers instead, you may want to incorporate more pockets, and reserve the shady side for plants that don't need as much sun.

The height of the barrel can be reduced if required. The whole barrel is built using half-bricks, so choose bricks that break in half easily. The structure looks complicated, but it is in fact simple to build as the trammel (see page 46) seems to do all the work for you. Make the strawberry barrel something to be proud of—take care over the joints and don't skimp on the decorative pebbles pressed into the mortar.

Front View Showing the Foundation and Trammel

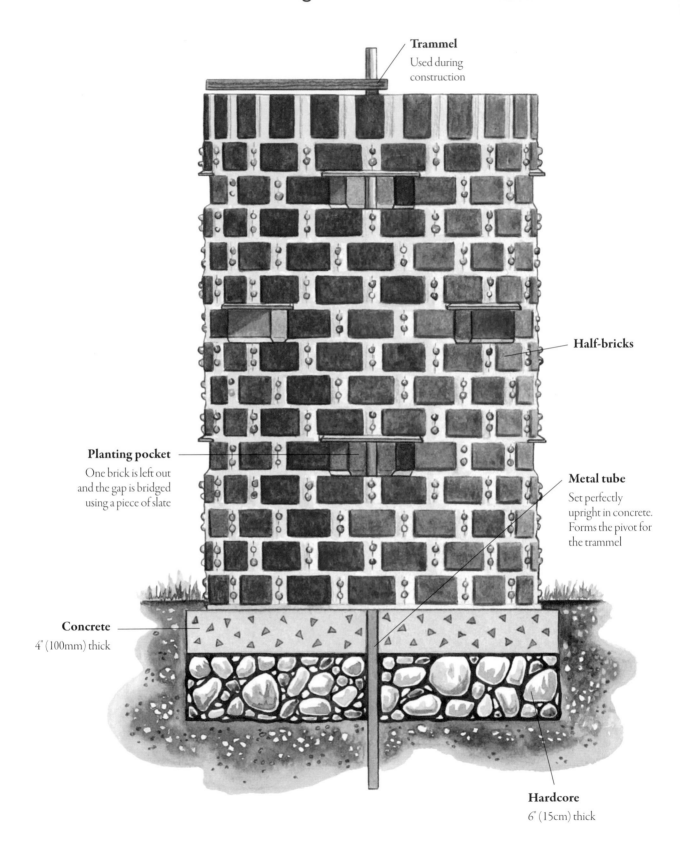

Trammel
Used during construction

Half-bricks

Planting pocket
One brick is left out and the gap is bridged using a piece of slate

Metal tube
Set perfectly upright in concrete. Forms the pivot for the trammel

Concrete
4" (100mm) thick

Hardcore
6" (15cm) thick

Exploded View of the Strawberry Barrel

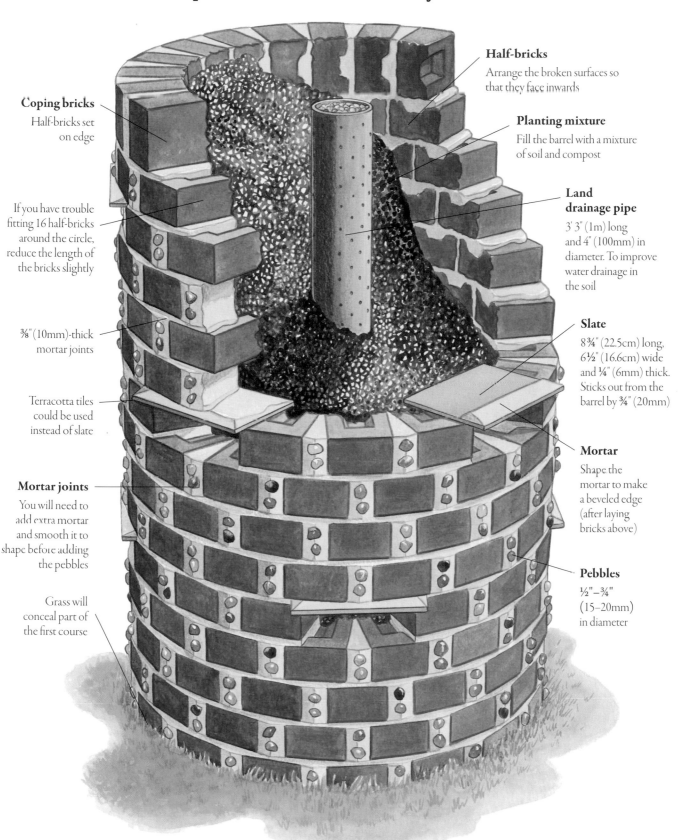

Half-bricks
Arrange the broken surfaces so that they face inwards

Coping bricks
Half-bricks set on edge

Planting mixture
Fill the barrel with a mixture of soil and compost

If you have trouble fitting 16 half-bricks around the circle, reduce the length of the bricks slightly

Land drainage pipe
3′ 3″ (1m) long and 4″ (100mm) in diameter. To improve water drainage in the soil

⅜″ (10mm)-thick mortar joints

Slate
8¾″ (22.5cm) long, 6½″ (16.6cm) wide and ¼″ (6mm) thick. Sticks out from the barrel by ¾″ (20mm)

Terracotta tiles could be used instead of slate

Mortar
Shape the mortar to make a beveled edge (after laying bricks above)

Mortar joints
You will need to add extra mortar and smooth it to shape before adding the pebbles

Pebbles
½″–¾″ (15–20mm) in diameter

Grass will conceal part of the first course

Plan View Showing the Trammel and a Complete Course of Bricks

Concrete

33¼" (84.5cm) square, 4" (100mm) thick. Set on 6" (15cm) of hardcore

Metal tube

Set perfectly upright in the concrete. Check that it is vertical by using a level

14¾" (37.6 mm)

Trammel arm

16¼" (41.2cm) long, 3" (65mm) wide and 1" (25mm) thick. Use the trammel to help you position the bricks accurately

Mortar

The wide gaps between the bricks need to be carefully filled with mortar

Plan View Showing the Layout of the Slates Over the Planting Pockets

Position the slate so that it sticks out from the side of the barrel by ¾" (20mm). Use the trammel as a guide

After each course of bricks, raise the trammel by 2½" (75mm) (the thickness of a brick plus ⅜" (10mm) of mortar) and support it at the center by clamping a pair of locking pliers underneath it

The slate should be placed centrally over the pocket of space beneath

Locking pliers
Slide up the tube until the trammel arm is at the correct height

Trammel arm
Establishes the correct position for the bricks

1 Build a level foundation. While the concrete is still wet, pound the metal tube into the center of the foundation. Check that it is vertical using the level. When the concrete is dry, make a trammel (see page 46). This trammel pivots on the metal tube. Use locking pliers to hold the trammel arm up. Practice laying the first course of half-bricks and check that you can fit sixteen around the circle.

Positioning
Set each brick square with the end of the trammel

Leveling
Tap the trammel until the brick is level

Drainage
The wood ensures an open joint for drainage

2 Mix up the mortar and start laying the first course of bricks, bedding them level on ⅜" (10mm)-thick mortar and using the trammel as a positional guide. Leave a scrap of wood between two of the bricks to create a water drainage hole (pull out on completion). Use the rubber mallet, on top of the end of the trammel arm, to knock the bricks down. Check that the course is level with the level.

3 Continue building further courses. After each course is complete, create angled mortar joints between the bricks and push two small pebbles into each one. This takes a bit of practice to get right, so be prepared to scrape out the first few joints and start over again.

Mortar

Angle a wedge of mortar between the bricks

Decoration

Push the pebbles into the soft mortar

Locking pliers

Slide the grips up until level with the slate

Slate

Push the slate outwards so that it overhangs by about ¾" (20mm)

4 Continue building upwards until you get to the fifth course. On this course, leave out four bricks to create the planting pockets. Cut pieces of slate or imitation slate and use these to bridge the gaps, the slate sticking out from the barrel by ¾" (20mm). After laying the next course, spread mortar over the part of the slate that sticks out.

Helpful Hint

Take care when fitting the pieces of slate—position them so that sharp edges face inwards, or smooth the edges and corners with an angle grinder. Clay tiles could be used instead of slate.

Soldier course

Arrange the half-bricks on their stretcher face for a decorative finish

5 After each course that includes planting pockets, lay three complete courses of bricks before the next course of planting pockets. After completing three courses with planting pockets, creating a total of twelve pockets, build a final course of bricks on top, followed by a soldier course. Fill all the joints with mortar, finish them with the pointing trowel, and stud with pebbles (not on the soldier course). After a few days, remove the metal tube by repeatedly bending it until it snaps off. Put a layer of clay pots in the bottom of the barrel for drainage, followed by the drainage pipe. Hold it upright as you fill the strawberry barrel with soil. Plant the pockets with strawberry plants.

SEMICIRCULAR STEPS

You might think that a doorstep is just a block of brickwork that enables you to move easily from one level to another, but that is only part of its function. Front doorsteps are traditionally built to make a grand, welcoming feature. The curved form of these steps makes attractive terracing, where there is plenty of space to set out a display of potted plants to make the entrance to the house look even more appealing.

⏱ TIME

Four days to build (five if you need a foundation).

Special Tips

Ensure that the surface of the steps is smooth, with no slightly raised areas that might cause people to trip. The steps must be correctly spaced for your site. (See page 53.)

YOU WILL NEED

For semicircular steps 7' 1" (2.16m) long, 3' 5" (1.04m) wide and 11¾" (29.8cm) high

Materials

- Bricks: 168
- Hardcore: 9 cu. feet (0.25 cu. meters)
- Concrete: 1 part (220 lbs., or 100kg) cement; 4 parts (880 lbs., or 400kg) ballast
- Mortar: 1 part (44 lbs., or 20kg) cement and 4 parts (175 lbs., 80kg) sand
- Wood for straightedge and trammel: 1 piece, 9' 10" (3m) long, 2" (35mm) wide and 1" (20mm) thick
- Wood for tamping beams: 1 piece, 12" (30cm) long and 3" (75mm) square, and 1 piece, 17¾" (45cm) long, 4" (100mm) wide and 2" (50mm) thick
- Masonry nails: 2 x 5" (14.5cm) (trammel pivot and guide)

🛠 Tools

- Tape measure and chalk
- Spade
- Wheelbarrow and bucket
- Shovel and mixing board, or cement mixer
- Sledgehammer
- Claw hammer
- Level
- Bricklayer's trowel and pointing trowel
- Bricklayer's hammer, brick chisel

A STEP UP FROM THE REST

First impressions count—or at least that is what people say when they meet somebody new—and the same applies to the entrance to your house. These decorative steps, with an interesting patterned surface, will definitely make a good impression, and their generous size provides a comfortable standing area.

When planning steps, one of the most important factors is the height of each step (the riser measurement). Steps should be no greater than 9" (23cm) high, and no less than 2⅜" (60mm) high (a good average would be 6", or 15cm).

You may need to adjust the design to suit your site (see page 53 about planning steps). If you have a paved surface surrounding the area of the steps, consider how you will repair it after the job is finished.

Mark out and build a concrete foundation that slopes away from the house slightly (about 1" per 6' 6", or 25mm per 2m): remove existing paving and dig a foundation 8" (20cm) deep, fill it with compacted hardcore 4" (100mm) thick, and top with 4" (100mm) of concrete.

Cross-Section Detail of the Semicircular Steps

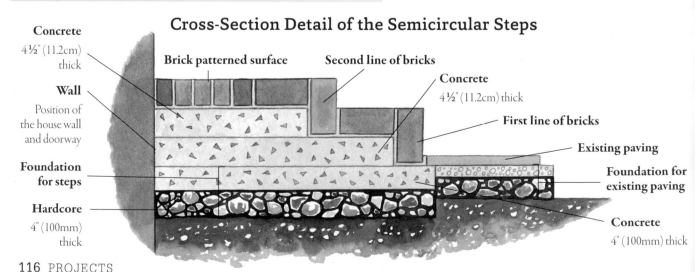

Concrete
4½" (11.2cm) thick

Wall
Position of the house wall and doorway

Foundation for steps

Hardcore
4" (100mm) thick

Brick patterned surface

Second line of bricks

Concrete
4½" (11.2cm) thick

First line of bricks

Existing paving

Foundation for existing paving

Concrete
4" (100mm) thick

Plan View of the Semicircular Steps

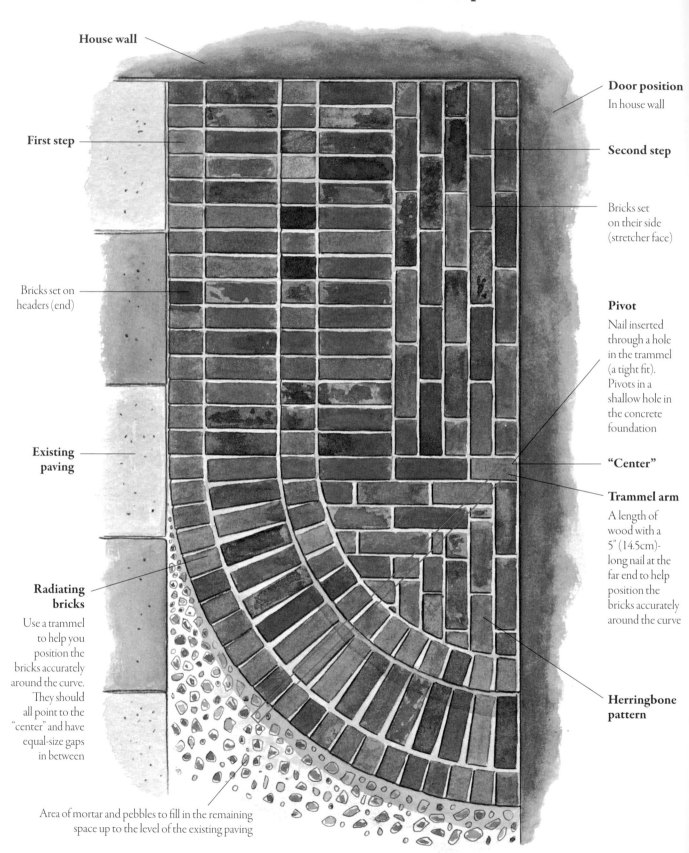

House wall

Door position
In house wall

First step

Second step

Bricks set
on their side
(stretcher face)

Bricks set on
headers (end)

Pivot
Nail inserted
through a hole
in the trammel
(a tight fit).
Pivots in a
shallow hole in
the concrete
foundation

**Existing
paving**

"Center"

Trammel arm
A length of
wood with a
5" (14.5cm)-
long nail at the
far end to help
position the
bricks accurately
around the curve

**Radiating
bricks**
Use a trammel
to help you
position the
bricks accurately
around the curve.
They should
all point to the
"center" and have
equal-size gaps
in between

**Herringbone
pattern**

Area of mortar and pebbles to fill in the remaining
space up to the level of the existing paving

Exploded View of the Semicircular Steps

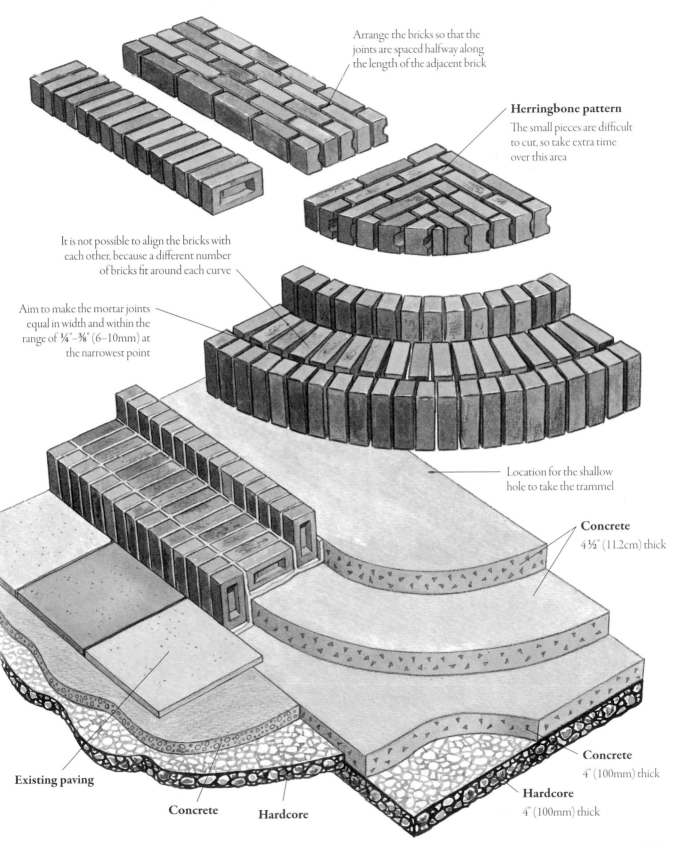

Arrange the bricks so that the joints are spaced halfway along the length of the adjacent brick

Herringbone pattern
The small pieces are difficult to cut, so take extra time over this area

It is not possible to align the bricks with each other, because a different number of bricks fit around each curve

Aim to make the mortar joints equal in width and within the range of ¼"–⅜" (6–10mm) at the narrowest point

Location for the shallow hole to take the trammel

Concrete
4½" (11.2cm) thick

Concrete
4" (100mm) thick

Hardcore
4" (100mm) thick

Existing paving

Concrete

Hardcore

Trammel
Has a hanging nail to facilitate the aligning of the bricks

Soldier bricks
Set the bricks upright on their header face

1 Build the outer edge of the bottom step from soldier bricks set on end, using the trammel (see page 46) and level to guide you. Butter the frog face with mortar, and lay each brick on ⅜" (10mm) of mortar. The straight bricks have ⅜" (10mm) of mortar between them, and the bricks following the curve have a minimum of ⅜" (10mm) of mortar between them.

Outer edge of bottom step
Area within is filled with concrete

Concrete
Depth must allow for (on top) a brick on its side plus ⅜" (10mm)

Tamping
Use scrap wood to tamp the concrete level

2 Fill the area within the outer edge with concrete to a level depth that leaves room for a layer of bricks on their stretcher face plus ⅜" (10mm) of mortar. Use the shorter tamping beam to spread the concrete and check that it is level. If in doubt, it is better to err on the side of having the concrete a bit lower (and later use extra mortar to build up the bricks to the correct level). Leave the concrete to dry.

3 Spread a bed of mortar over the concrete and use the trammel and level to help you lay the curve of bricks. The gaps between the bricks won't line up with the outer edge, but try to maintain equal-thickness gaps, and make sure all the bricks around the curve point to the "center" (see working drawing).

Alignment
The bricks must point towards the "center" of the trammel

4 Build the outer edge of the top step on the same slab of concrete and again use the trammel to guide you around the curve. Check that the tops of the bricks are level with the bottom of the doorway. Allow the mortar between the bricks to dry before proceeding to the next stage.

Step level
Ensure that the soldier bricks are upright

Trammel
Check the alignment of every brick

Concrete

Depth must allow for (on top) a brick on its side plus ⅜" (10mm)

Tamping

Tamp the concrete level

Brick level

Keep checking that the bricks remain true

5 Fill the area inside the outer edge of the top step with concrete as described in step 2. Tamp with the longer tamping beam. There should be enough space to lay the final bricks on a ⅜" (10mm)-thick bed of mortar.

Pattern
This area of pattern is what people will notice first when they approach your door. If you are worried about fitting the bricks into the space, or think you might make a mistake, practice setting out the bricks in the design before spreading mortar

6 When the concrete has set, fill in the top step with bricks in the two patterns illustrated. Lay the straight line of staggered bricks first, then finish with the 90° pattern that fills the curved area. Cut the bricks to shape using the bricklayer's hammer or club hammer and brick chisel. Fill the joints with a dryish mixture of mortar and clean them up with the pointing trowel.

Helpful Hint

When you are leveling the bricks, try to make them end up sloping away from the house slightly.

TUDOR ARCH WALL NICHE

A niche in a wall always invites questions. What is it for? Is it a shrine? Is it a blocked-up window? When was it built? So if you want to create a bit of intrigue in your garden, this project is ideal. In Tudor times in England, bricks first came to be used in a decorative way, and this niche has been inspired by Tudor arches. It is an exciting but complex project to build—an enjoyably skill-testing challenge.

⏱ TIME

Six days (do not lay more than four courses in one day).

Special Tips

See page 50 for information on walls and requirements for piers and buttresses.

YOU WILL NEED

For Tudor arch wall niche 5' 3" (1.61m) high and 4' 9" (1.45m) wide

Materials

- Bricks: 276
- Stone slab: 1 piece, 21¾" (55.4cm) long, 9¾" (25cm) wide and 1½" (40mm) thick (sill)
- Hardcore: 3½ cu. feet (0.1 cu. meters)
- Sand: 1 shovelful
- Concrete: 1 part (66 lbs., or 30kg) cement and 4 parts (265 lbs., or 120kg) ballast
- Nails: 20 x 1½" (40mm)
- Mortar: 1 part (66 lbs., or 30kg) cement and 4 parts (265 lbs., or 120kg) sand
- Wood for sticks for center of former: 10 pieces, 3¼" (85mm) long, 2" (30mm) wide and 1" (22mm) thick
- Wood for trammel: 1 piece, 27½" (70cm) long, 2" (35mm) wide and 1" (22mm) thick
- Plywood for former: 2 pieces, 22" (56.3cm) long, 4¾" (12.2cm) wide and ¼" (6mm) thick

Tools

- Tape measure, stakes, string, straightedge and piece of chalk
- Spade
- Wheelbarrow and bucket
- Shovel and mixing board, or cement mixer
- Bricklayer's trowel and pointing trowel
- Bricklayer's hammer and club hammer
- Brick chisel
- Rubber mallet
- Level
- General-purpose saw
- Jigsaw
- Claw hammer
- Sledgehammer

A FINE DISPLAY

The recess or niche is decorative in itself, but it also acts like a picture frame for anything you want to display in it. We have put a statuette in this one, but yours could display a mosaic picture, salvaged wagon wheel or curious antique. Other ideas include a wall mask fixed in the recess, spouting water into a stone trough, or the whole arch can be built deeper and bigger and the sill made into a narrow seat for perching on—a kind of brick arbor.

This project is a little more challenging than the others, because you need to keep all the vertical joints in the coursework aligned. This ensures that the sides of the archway are well presented. However, the finished results are well worth the effort.

Front View of the Tudor Arch Wall Niche

Coping
Soldier bricks

Arch

Niche
A recess 27¼" (69.5cm) high and 22½" (57.3cm) wide

Sill
9¾" (25cm) wide (front to back)

Concrete
5" (12.5cm) thick

Hardcore
8" (20cm) thick

Exploded View of the Tudor Arch Wall Niche

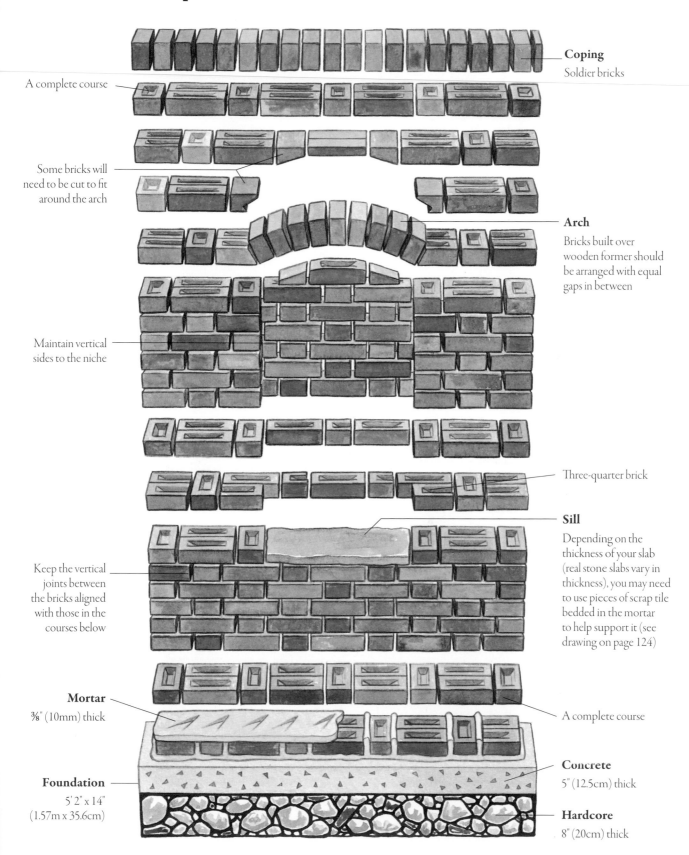

Coping
Soldier bricks

A complete course

Some bricks will need to be cut to fit around the arch

Arch
Bricks built over wooden former should be arranged with equal gaps in between

Maintain vertical sides to the niche

Three-quarter brick

Sill
Depending on the thickness of your slab (real stone slabs vary in thickness), you may need to use pieces of scrap tile bedded in the mortar to help support it (see drawing on page 124)

Keep the vertical joints between the bricks aligned with those in the courses below

Mortar
⅜" (10mm) thick

A complete course

Foundation
5' 2" x 14"
(1.57m x 35.6cm)

Concrete
5" (12.5cm) thick

Hardcore
8" (20cm) thick

Wall

Build a base wall
to the required
sill height

Bond

Flemish bond
results in an
extremely
strong bond

1 Build a foundation
5' 2" (1.57m) long and
14" (35.6cm) wide, consisting
of an 8" (20cm)-thick layer
of hardcore topped with a
5" (12.5cm)-thick layer of
concrete. When the concrete is
dry, lay the first course of bricks.
Note that this wall is two bricks
thick, and is built using Flemish
bond. Continue building the wall
until you have completed seven
courses. Use a straightedge, level
and rubber mallet to help double-
check the level and straightness of
the wall. Scrape out and clean the
joints before the mortar dries.

Leveling

Use mortar,
and if necessary
scraps of slate,
to ensure the sill
is level

2 On the eighth course, leave
a central space for the slab.
Check that your stone sill is the
correct size by placing it on the
wall. The ends should align with
joints between the bricks of the
sixth course (if not, cut to size).
Position the slab on a generous
bed of mortar and coat it with
sand to protect the surface during
the rest of the building operation.
The slab protrudes from the wall
by 1⅜" (36mm).

Sill

Ease the sill
outwards so that
it protrudes by
1⅜" (36mm)

Single-thickness wall
Use half-bricks to create the illusion of a Flemish bond

Corners
Make sure that the corners are vertically true

Former
The former can be rough and ready, as long as it does the job

Plywood
Draw the shape of the former by using a grid to plot the curve, or use a trammel to draw an arc with a radius of 23⅝" (60cm)

Alignment
The curved pieces must be aligned with each other

3 Continue building upwards for a further eight courses, reducing the wall to a single thickness at the back of the slab, creating a niche. Study the working drawings to see how the bricks are placed for the best effect.

4 Build a wooden former to support the arch during construction. (See page 46 for information about trammels.) Cut out the pieces with the jigsaw and join together—place one of the sticks underneath and hammer through the plywood into the stick. Nail on the rest of the sticks in the same way, then put the other sheet of plywood on top, and nail through into the sticks.

Practice
It is a good idea to practice arranging bricks on top of the former. Once you have a feel for the gaps it is necessary to leave between each brick, it is more likely that you will arrange them correctly when building with mortar. Angle them so they are all aimed at a central point on the sill

5 Support the former on piles of bricks. Continue building the single-brick-thick wall behind it, cutting bricks to follow the shape of the curve. Complete the course either side of the arch using angled bricks to support it (see diagram). Lay the top of the arch over the former, maintaining equal gaps between the bricks. Build two courses above the arch, cutting bricks as necessary. Finish with a soldier brick coping.

Helpful Hint
You risk damaging the formwork if you knock the bricks too hard. It is better to take your time applying the correct amount of mortar to each brick.

CLASSIC ROUND POND

There is something complete and rather satisfying about a circular pool of water. This sunken pond is interesting to build and makes a beautiful feature that will suit most styles of garden. We have built it to fit snugly into a patio, where it can be surrounded by an ever-changing display of container plants to give the pond a distinct seasonal character.

 TIME

Two days to dig the hole and four to five days to complete the brickwork.

Special Tips

If you have young children, it is better not to have a pond in your garden.

YOU WILL NEED

For a pond 6' 7" (2.02m) in diameter and 36" (90cm) deep

 Materials

- Bricks: 220 (walls) and 47 (top edge)
- Concrete: 1 part (160 lbs., or 72kg) cement and 4 parts (635 lbs., or 288kg) ballast
- Mortar: 1 part (110 lbs., or 50kg) cement and 3 parts (330 lbs., or 150kg) sand
- Builder's sand: 1 ton
- Nails: 5 x 2½" (60mm)
- Wood for tamping beam with handles: 1 piece, 6' 3" (1.9m) long, 4" (90mm) wide and 3" (60mm thick, and 2 pieces, 3' 11" (1.2m) long, 4" (90mm) wide and 2" (30mm) thick
- Wood for trammel support block: 1 piece, 8" (20cm) long,

- 3" (75mm) wide and 3" (75mm) thick
- Wood for trammel arm: 1 piece, 4' 3" (1.29m) long, 3" (65mm) wide and 2" (30mm) thick
- Wood for beam to check level: 1 piece, 6' (1.84m) long, 4" (90mm) wide and 2" (30mm) thick
- Plywood for trammel: 1 piece, 20" (50cm) square and ¼" (6mm) thick (base), and 1 piece, 18⅜" (46.7cm) long, 12" (30.5cm) wide and ¼" (6mm) thick (U-shaped piece)
- Geotextile: 400 sq. feet (37 sq. meters)
- Butyl liner: 1 piece, 15' (4.3m) square

 **Tools**

- Tape measure, stakes, string, marking chalk or spray marker
- Spade and fork
- Wheelbarrow and bucket
- Scissors
- General-purpose saw
- Claw hammer

- Shovel and mixing board, or cement mixer
- Jigsaw
- Portable workbench
- Bricklayer's trowel and pointing trowel
- Bricklayer's hammer
- Level
- Sledgehammer

CIRCLE POWER

This round, sunken brick pond is a classic. A pond often becomes the focal point of a garden or yard, and can be treated in different ways—you can populate it with fish, plant a glorious display of water-lilies, or install a water feature.

There are important safety factors to take into account if you are considering building a pond. If you have young children, it is safer not to have a pond. (To protect visiting children, make a slatted wooden lid to cover the pond for short periods.)

Avoid excavating areas where there is a likelihood of uncovering pipes and drains—as a general rule, always dig carefully and if you encounter any, seek expert advice. (See also page 62.) If you want to install a fountain, incorporate armored plastic pipe (2" (50mm) in diameter) to protect the pump cable, which will run across the bottom of the pond (on top of the liner), through a hole in the wall, up between the wall and the liner, over the edge of the liner, and then be buried under paving slabs.

Layout of the First Course of Bricks

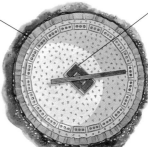

Pond lining
A combination of butyl and geotextile runs under the concrete foundation and up behind the wall

Trammel
Use a length of wood pivoted at the center of the pond to indicate the correct positioning of the wall bricks (see also page 46)

Layout of the Top Edge Bricks

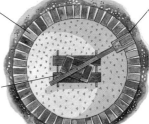

Edge bricks
These are laid with equal-size gaps in between

Portable workbench
Supports trammel

Trammel
The same setup as above, but extended using a piece of plywood with the shape of a brick cut out of it

Cut-Away Cross-Section View of the Classic Round Pond

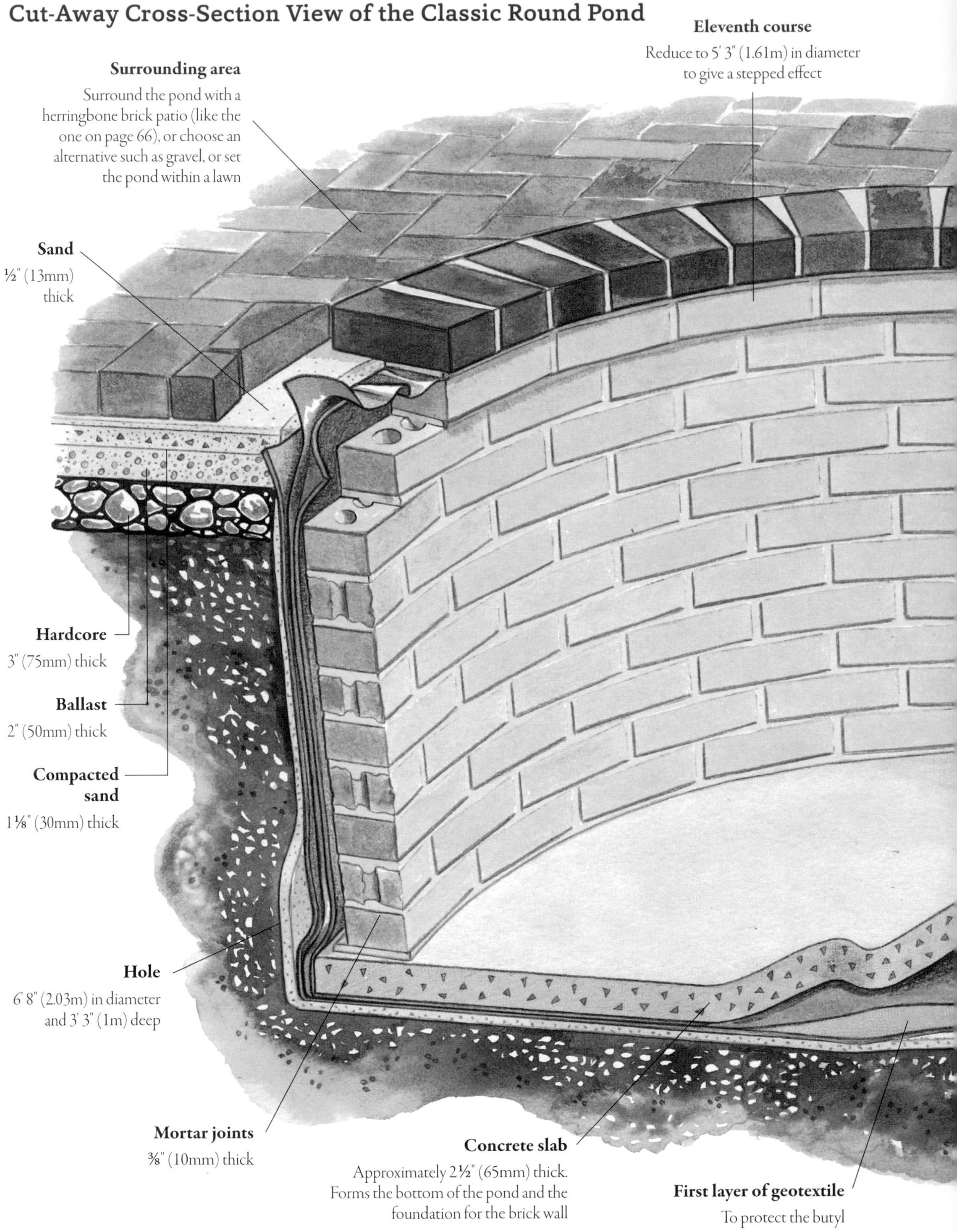

Surrounding area
Surround the pond with a herringbone brick patio (like the one on page 66), or choose an alternative such as gravel, or set the pond within a lawn

Eleventh course
Reduce to 5' 3" (1.61m) in diameter to give a stepped effect

Sand
½" (13mm) thick

Hardcore
3" (75mm) thick

Ballast
2" (50mm) thick

Compacted sand
1⅛" (30mm) thick

Hole
6' 8" (2.03m) in diameter and 3' 3" (1m) deep

Mortar joints
⅜" (10mm) thick

Concrete slab
Approximately 2½" (65mm) thick. Forms the bottom of the pond and the foundation for the brick wall

First layer of geotextile
To protect the butyl

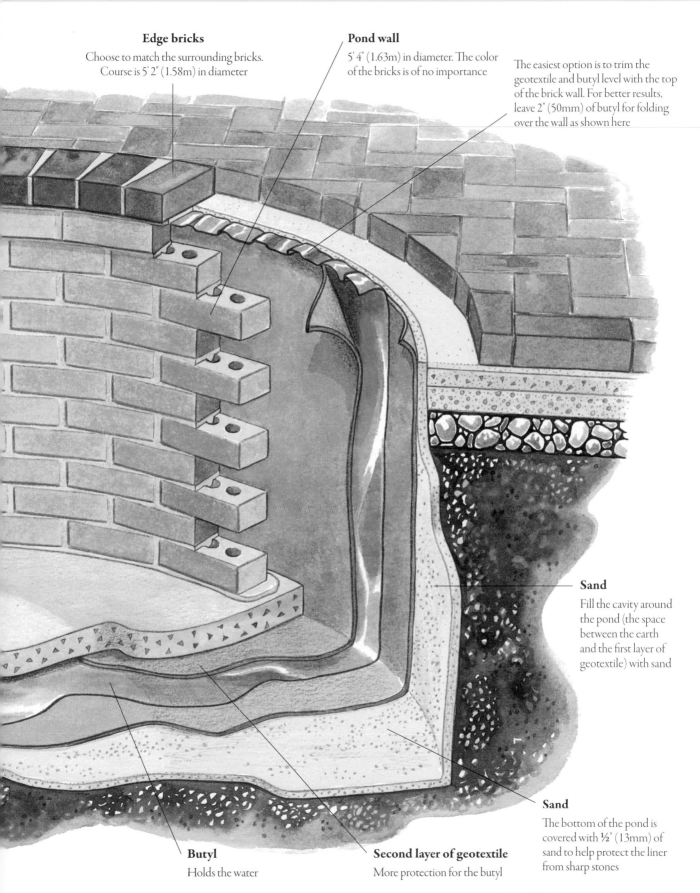

Edge bricks

Choose to match the surrounding bricks. Course is 5' 2" (1.58m) in diameter

Pond wall

5' 4" (1.63m) in diameter. The color of the bricks is of no importance

The easiest option is to trim the geotextile and butyl level with the top of the brick wall. For better results, leave 2" (50mm) of butyl for folding over the wall as shown here

Sand

Fill the cavity around the pond (the space between the earth and the first layer of geotextile) with sand

Sand

The bottom of the pond is covered with ½" (13mm) of sand to help protect the liner from sharp stones

Butyl

Holds the water

Second layer of geotextile

More protection for the butyl

Digging

Work slowly, so the sides of the hole don't collapse

Hole shape

If the earth at the sides crumbles, make the hole wider at the top

Top

Use bricks to hold the top of the textile in place

Sides

Be generous and allow a big overlap

Bottom

Remove sharp stones before laying the geotextile

1 Mark out a circle 6' 8" (2.03m) in diameter (and a patio area if required), and dig out the earth to a depth of 3' 3" (1m). The soil may crumble a little at the edges, but this is not a problem as long as the hole is at least 6' 8" (2.03m) in diameter at the bottom. If the ground is hard and rocky, break it up with a pickaxe or mattock.

2 Remove sharp stones from the hole and line it with sand followed by geotextile. Cover the bottom first and then drape it up the sides, with evenly distributed folds and overlaps of 4" (100mm) or more at the joins. Make sure that it overlaps the top of the hole by at least 12" (30cm). Weigh down the edges with bricks.

Butyl

Use bricks to hold the top edge in place

Sides

Try to distribute the folds equally around the sides

Geotextile

Cover the butyl with geotextile as in step 2

Tamping

Tamp the concrete level right up to the sides of the hole

Concrete

Lay a 2½" (65mm)- thick slab on top of the geotextile

3 Cover the geotextile with a single sheet of butyl. (Don't put water in the hole to help spread it.) Keep rearranging it so that it takes up the shape of the pond and the folds are evenly distributed. It should overlap the edge of the pond by at least 12" (30cm); weigh down the top edge with bricks.

4 Spread a second layer of geotextile over the butyl, overlap the edges and weigh it down. Ask a friend to help you lay a slab of 2½" (65mm)-thick concrete in the bottom of the pond, smoothing it out with a tamping beam (fix handles to the beam with nails) operated from ground level. Allow the concrete to dry for two days.

Horizontal level

Check the level of every course of bricks

Vertical level

Use the level to ensure that the walls are vertical and true

5 Build a round brick wall, ten bricks high, on top of the concrete (diameter is approx. 5' 4", or 1.63m). You may prefer to use a trammel to establish the circle (see pages 46 and 130). Allow ⅜" (10mm)-thick mortar joints, scrape away excess mortar and clean the joints before the mortar dries. Check vertical and horizontal levels during construction. Add an eleventh course, overlapping the previous one by about ⅝" (15mm), to give a decorative stepped edge to the pond (diameter is 5' 3", or 1.61m).

Trammel

Use a trammel to ensure that the edge forms a true circle

Patio

If you are going to surround the pond with a patio, dig out the earth around the pond. Spread 2" (50mm) of hardcore, 1⅛" (30mm) of compacted ballast, and ½" (13mm) of uncompacted course sand over the area

6 Fold the pond lining (geotextile and butyl) over the wall and into the pond. Fill the cavity between the wall and the earth with sand. Trim the pond lining level with the bricks. Make a trammel (or if you used one in step 5, adjust it) that indicates a circle 5' 2" (1.58m) in diameter, and lay the twelfth course of bricks around the edge of the pond. The trammel consists of a plywood base, placed on a workbench. The base holds the trammel support block, surrounded by bricks to keep it in place and weigh down the base. The trammel arm pivots on a nail in the trammel support block. A U-shaped trammel piece is fixed to the trammel arm to indicate the position of the edge bricks, which are laid to meet the end of the trammel at 90°. Finish work on the surrounding area.

BRICK BARBECUE

This impressive structure beats other barbecues hands down in terms of attractiveness and practicality. There is a huge area for cooking, large work surfaces, a couple of handy shelves, and a hearth chimney for the smoke. It makes an eye-catching garden feature, and out of barbecue season, the work surfaces and shelves would be good for displaying plants (place containers on saucers to avoid staining the surfaces).

⏱ TIME

Five days (assuming there is an existing foundation).

Special Tips

Do not leave a lit barbecue unattended, especially if you have young children and pets.

YOU WILL NEED

For a barbecue 5' 3" (1.61m) high, 5' 1" (1.56m) wide and 33" (83.2cm) deep

Materials

- Bricks: 377
- Concrete slabs: 4 slabs, 17⅜" (44.1cm) square and 1⅛" (30mm) thick
- Tiles: 30 tiles, 6" (15cm) square and ⁵⁄₁₆" (8mm) thick
- Slate: 6 random, fairly oval pieces, about 2" (50mm) in diameter and ⁵⁄₁₆" (8mm) thick
- Mortar: 1 part (88 lbs., or 40kg) cement and 4 parts (350 lbs., or 160kg) sand
- Wood for sticks for center of former: 9 pieces, 7½" (19.2cm) long, 2" (35mm) wide and 1" (22mm) thick

- Wood for trammel: 1 piece, 18" (46cm) long, 2" (35mm) wide and 1" (22mm) thick
- Wood for straightedge: 1 piece, 5' 7" (1.7m) long, 2" (35mm) wide and 1" (20mm) thick
- Plywood for former: 2 pieces, 28" (72cm) long, 14¼" (36cm) wide and ¼" (6mm) thick
- Nails: 18 x 1¼" (30mm)
- Grill kit: between 25"–27" x 13¾"–17¾" (64–68.5cm x 34.8–45cm)

Tools

- Tape measure, straightedge and piece of chalk
- Spade, fork and shovel
- Wheelbarrow and bucket
- Sledgehammer
- Shovel and mixing board, or cement mixer
- Jigsaw

- Bricklayer's trowel and pointing trowel
- Bricklayer's hammer and club hammer
- Brick chisel
- Rubber mallet
- Level
- General-purpose saw
- Claw hammer

EATING OUT

Everyone enjoys a barbecue—there is something very appealing about cooking and eating food outdoors in warm weather. This barbecue is ideal if you do a lot of entertaining, because it is bigger than average and built to last. It will banish forever those barbecuing balancing acts with tiny, feeble contraptions that seem to rust as you look at them.

Take considerable care when deciding on a location for the barbecue. It is obviously not feasible to move the completed structure, so before committing to a spot, have a trial cooking session there on a disposable barbecue. Watch out for hazards such as low branches, or plants growing on a pergola overhead that might shrivel in the heat or catch fire, and drawbacks such as being just too far away from the seating area. The barbecue needs a firm foundation, so check what is under your existing patio (see page 35) or build a new foundation as shown on page 138.

Perspective View of the Brick Barbecue

Decorative chimney archway

Concrete slabs Provide plenty of working area

Supports for a grill kit

Build on a patio or construct a special foundation

Plan View Showing the Layout of the First Course of Bricks

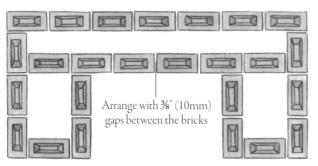

Arrange with ⅜" (10mm) gaps between the bricks

Plan View Showing the Layout of the Second Course of Bricks

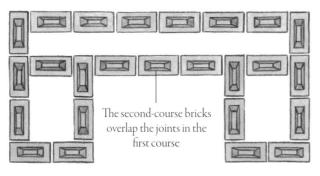

The second-course bricks overlap the joints in the first course

Plan View Showing the Layout of the Seventh Course of Bricks

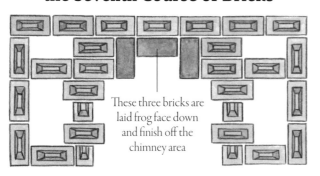

These three bricks are laid frog face down and finish off the chimney area

Plan View Showing the Layout of the Ninth Course of Bricks

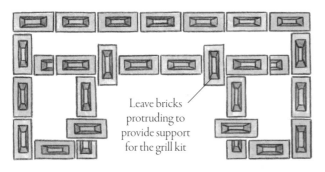

Leave bricks protruding to provide support for the grill kit

Front View of the Arch Former (One Side Removed)

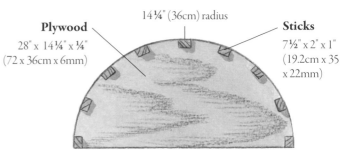

Plywood
28" x 14¼" x ¼"
(72 x 36cm x 6mm)

14¼" (36cm) radius

Sticks
7½" x 2" x 1"
(19.2cm x 35 x 22mm)

Perspective View of the Arch Former

Make sure sides are in alignment

Fix with 1¼" (30mm) nails

Side View of the Brick Barbecue

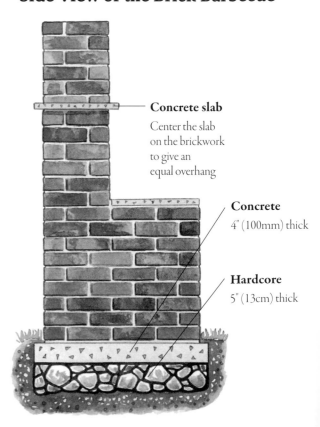

Concrete slab
Center the slab on the brickwork to give an equal overhang

Concrete
4" (100mm) thick

Hardcore
5" (13cm) thick

Exploded View of the Brick Barbecue

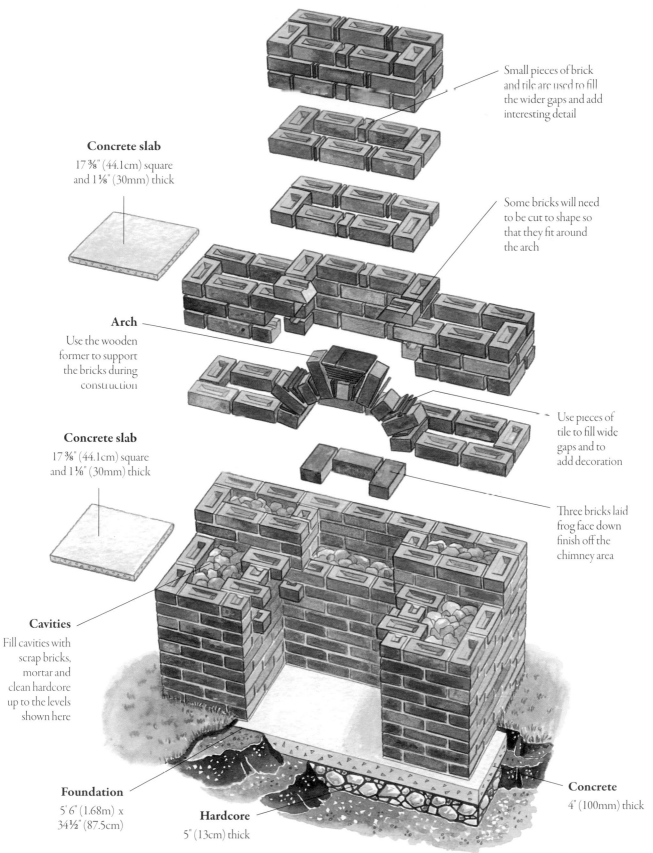

Small pieces of brick and tile are used to fill the wider gaps and add interesting detail

Concrete slab
17 ⅜" (44.1cm) square and 1⅛" (30mm) thick

Some bricks will need to be cut to shape so that they fit around the arch

Arch
Use the wooden former to support the bricks during construction

Concrete slab
17 ⅜" (44.1cm) square and 1⅛" (30mm) thick

Use pieces of tile to fill wide gaps and to add decoration

Three bricks laid frog face down finish off the chimney area

Cavities
Fill cavities with scrap bricks, mortar and clean hardcore up to the levels shown here

Foundation
5' 6" (1.68m) x 34½" (87.5cm)

Hardcore
5" (13cm) thick

Concrete
4" (100mm) thick

First course
Spend time perfecting the layout

Guidelines
Draw around the layout with chalk

1 If you do not have an existing patio area that provides a firm foundation on which to build, dig a 9" (23cm)-deep hole and lay 5" (13cm) of compacted hardcore and 4" (100mm) of concrete (add 2" (50mm) to the depth of the hole if the barbecue will be surrounded by grass—this allows the bricks to merge into the grass). Mark out the outer area of the barbecue and practice arranging your first course of bricks (without mortar) in the order shown. Check that the grill and tray fit.

Mortar
Use a fairly stiff mortar for the first course

Squareness
It is vital that the angles are at 90°

Leveling
Make adjustments to ensure that the bricks are level

2 If you are working on an existing patio, check that it is level in all directions before proceeding. If it does slope, it can probably be compensated for by adding extra mortar in the first course. If the slope is too great (more than ⅜" (10mm) across the length of the barbecue), you will need to cast a level concrete slab on top, at least 1½" (40mm) thick. Begin laying the first course of bricks.

3 Continue building up the walls, making sure all the joints are staggered and that the structure is level and vertical. Check each brick with the level before proceeding to the next, and take time to finish off the joints between bricks before the mortar dries.

Corners
As you build the corners, check that they are true with the level

Waste
All the brick and mortar leftovers can be put into the cavities

Supports
Center the support bricks across the thickness of the wall

Levels
Ensure the support bricks are level with each other

4 Complete six courses, and on the seventh course change the layout of bricks as shown, so that four bricks stick out into the recess. The ends of these bricks provide support for the metal tray.

Grill
The grill will finish up two courses higher than the tray

Levels
Make adjustments to ensure the grill and tray are level and parallel with each other

5 Continue building upward and incorporate support for the grill in the ninth course. Check that both the tray and grill fit in the recess, and then put them aside. At this stage, the brickwork either side of the recess is complete and you can now concentrate on the back of the barbecue. Make a wooden former to support the brickwork arch as in the Tudor Arch Wall Niche project on pages 124–129.

Arch
Use mortar and slate to correct the angle of bricks around the arch

Former
Propped up on bricks

Supports
Use thin bits of wood or slate to level the former

6 Prop up the former on bricks. Build the arch over it, using pieces of slate to help prop up the bricks over the arch. Starting from one side, put mortar on the bricks that are already there, then place one of the arch bricks, making sure it is pointing to the center of the arch (if not, push a piece of slate underneath to prop it to the correct angle). Continue laying bricks around the arch, and when you are almost at the center, start at the other side. Finish by inserting a central brick.

Courses
Make sure the bricks are level each side of the arch

Tiles
Use broken tiles to make decorative infills

7 Fill the cavities in the barbecue, up to the the level of the grill, with scrap bricks, mortar and clean hardcore. Fill in the area over the arch with bricks cut to size and pieces of decorative tile. Use the pointing trowel to fill any gaps and touch up the mortar joints as you build.

Levels
Make repeated checks with the level

Work surfaces
Use mortar and slate to level the slabs

8 Complete building the chimney stack, checking levels as you work. Check that the concrete slab surfaces fit and bed them level on a ⅜" (10mm)-thick layer of mortar. Finish off all the mortar joints. Wait a few days before having a barbecue, or the heat will dry out the mortar too quickly.

FEATURE WALL

An ancient brick wall is a unique piece of history, as well as a charming structure. It is a record of changing needs—as time passes, doors and windows are altered and filled in with bits of this and that. This project aims to achieve a similar patchwork of interesting features. If you wish, you can make it as a piece of art that reflects your own personal history, with structures and textures to represent significant events in your own life, such as marriage or the birth of a child.

⏱ TIME

Six days (do not lay more than four courses in a day).

Special Tips

Add a buttress behind the wall to make it safer if you have children (see page 50).

YOU WILL NEED

For a wall 7½' (1.71m) high and 8' 6" (2.58m) long

Materials

- Bricks: 306
- Stone slab: 1, 17" (43cm) long, 9½" (24cm) wide and 2⅜" (60mm) thick
- Stone boulders: 2, 8" (20cm) in diameter
- Stone, 14 small pieces: 12" (30cm) long, 8" (20cm) wide and 1⅛" (30mm) thick
- Millstone: 16" (41cm) in diameter and 4⅜" (11cm) thick
- Tiles: 9 tiles, 8½" (21.5cm) long, 6⅜" (16.2cm) wide and ⅜" (10mm) thick
- Cobblestones: 40 cobblestones, 2" (50mm) in diameter
- Pebbles: 150 pebbles, ½" (15mm) in diameter
- Hardcore: 7 cu. feet (0.2 cu. meters)

- Concrete: 1 part (133 lbs., or 60kg) cement and 4 parts (530 lbs., or 240kg) ballast
- Mortar: 1 part (133 lbs., or 60kg) cement and 4 parts (530 lbs., or 240kg) sand
- Wood for sticks for center of former: 8 pieces, 8" (20.4cm) long, 2" (35mm) wide and 1" (22mm) thick
- Wood for trammel: 1 piece, 22" (56cm) long, 2" (35mm) wide and 1" (22mm) thick
- Plywood for former: 2 pieces, 18⅛" (46cm) long, 15½" (39.5cm) wide and ¼" (6mm) thick
- Nails: 16 x 1½" (40mm)

Tools

- Tape measure, stakes, string, straightedge and a piece of chalk
- Spade and fork
- Wheelbarrow and bucket
- Sledgehammer
- Shovel and mixing board, or cement mixer
- Claw hammer

- Bricklayer's trowel and pointing trowel
- Bricklayer's hammer and club hammer
- Brick chisel
- Level
- General-purpose saw
- Jigsaw

TIME AND TEXTURE

There is something fascinating about walking through the ruins of a once-magnificent castle or abbey, and seeing crumbling archways held up as if by magic, and staircases that lead nowhere. Wouldn't it be great to have your own mysterious ruin at the bottom of the garden? Well, now is your chance to build something unusual with a historical feel.

This wall is 7' 6" (1.71m) high, and so needs a strong foundation as illustrated on page 146. We haven't built reinforcing piers or buttresses, because the wall is at the bottom of the garden beside a hedge and is unlikely to be disturbed, but if you have children who are likely to play nearby, you must include extra support (see supporting piers and buttresses on page 50).

All sorts of brick and stone materials can be built into this wall, so don't feel that you have to follow the drawings exactly. Pieces of carved stone, fossils or even shells would also look great bedded in the mortar.

Plan View Showing the First Course of Bricks

Foundation
8' 8" x 12" (2.65m x 30cm)

Two-brick-thick wall
Laid in a Flemish bond

Plan View Showing the Second Course of Bricks

In the second course, the bricks are laid so that they overlap the joints in the first course

Front View of the Arch Former (One Side Removed)

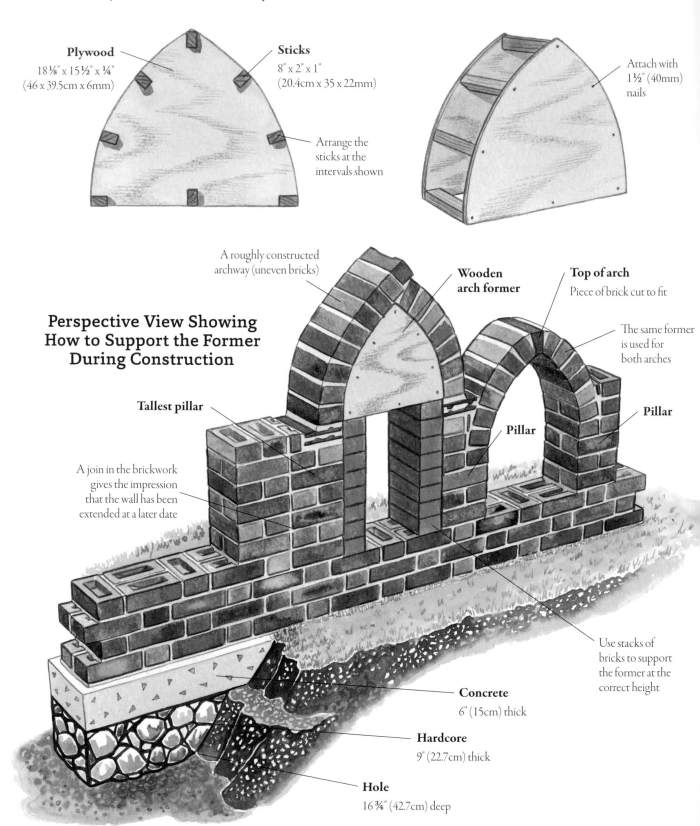

Plywood
18 ⅛" x 15 ½" x ¼"
(46 x 39.5cm x 6mm)

Sticks
8" x 2" x 1"
(20.4cm x 35 x 22mm)

Arrange the sticks at the intervals shown

Perspective View of the Arch Former

Attach with 1½" (40mm) nails

A roughly constructed archway (uneven bricks)

Wooden arch former

Top of arch
Piece of brick cut to fit

The same former is used for both arches

Perspective View Showing How to Support the Former During Construction

Tallest pillar

Pillar

Pillar

A join in the brickwork gives the impression that the wall has been extended at a later date

Use stacks of bricks to support the former at the correct height

Concrete
6" (15cm) thick

Hardcore
9" (22.7cm) thick

Hole
16 ¾" (42.7cm) deep

Exploded View of the Feature Wall

Coping
Soldier course

A complete course

Whole brick

Decorative course

Half brick

A complete course

Cut bricks to fit around archway

Leave unfinished edges to give the appearance of a tumbledown ruin

Stone
Random pieces, no bigger than 12" x 8" x 1⅛" (30 x 20cm x 30mm)

Millstone
16" (41cm) in diameter and 4⅜" (11cm) thick

Tile
8½" x 6⅜" x ⅜" (21.5 x 16.2cm x 10mm)

Cobblestones
2" (50mm) in diameter

Boulders
8" (20cm) in diameter

Stone slab
17" x 9½" x 2⅜" (43 x 24cm x 60mm)

Levels

Use the level to check the levels

Bond

Use a Flemish bond to build the wall three courses high

1 Dig a foundation hole 16¾" (42.7cm) deep, and lay 9" (22.7cm) of compacted hardcore and 6" (15cm) of concrete. Use chalk and a mason's string line or straightedge to mark the position of the wall. Build three courses of bricks in the decorative bond shown. Make sure all the vertical joints are staggered and check that the wall is level and vertical. The finished wall is meant to look like an old structure that has been repaired many times over the years, so just finish the joints by scraping out excess mortar and don't bother filling gaps.

Level

Ensure the pillars are upright and parallel

Levels

Ensure the pillars are level with each other

Pillar

Build two, two-by-two brick pillars

2 Build up two brick pillars (as shown here) and a third, taller pillar (as shown in the drawings on pages 146–147). Make sure all the bricks are turned so that they overlap the joints of the bricks below and check that they are level using the level.

Former
Refer to the working drawings for the shape of the former

3 Make a wooden former to support the brickwork arch. You can draw the shape of the arch on the plywood using a trammel (see page 46) to make the two 18⅛" (46cm)-radius arcs. Cut out the arch shape with the jigsaw. Join the pieces together as shown in the Tudor Arch Wall Niche project on pages 124–129.

Top of arch
Use a piece of brick cut to fit

Soldier bricks
Lay bricks on their stretcher face over the former

Former
Propped up on bricks

4 Prop up the wooden former on piles of bricks between the two small pillars. Lay bricks up each side of the arch, leaving equal spaces between each brick and tapping them down with the handle of the bricklayer's hammer. At the top of the arch, lay a brick that has been cut to fit.

Bond

Continue the
Flemish bond
over the arch

Stepped detail

Use tiles to build
idiosyncratic
details

5 Build around the arch with brick and pieces of tile and stone as shown in the drawing (or according to your own design). This is a good way of using up spare bricks and stone. When the mortar has dried, remove the wooden former and reuse it to build the second (higher) arch. Fill in the lower arch with bricks and stone. Brick up the back of the higher arch, using a single thickness of bricks.

Top of arch

Bricks cut to fit

Detailing

Complete
the recess by
filling in around
the millstone
with mortar
and cobblestones

Infill

Fill the recess
with found items

6 Mortar the millstone in the recess of the higher arch and fill in around it with cobblestones and mortar. Interesting salvaged architectural features or broken pieces of earthenware could also be incorporated into the structure.

Soldier bricks

Top the wall with a coping of soldier bricks

7 Finish building the regular courses above the level of the arches and start on the decorative strips of bricks at the top. Cut bricks in half and use these for the recessed details. Complete the building process with a course of soldier bricks to form the coping.

Helpful Hint

You can make brickwork look old and weathered by scraping mortar from between the bricks, and then using a wire brush to erode the mortar before it dries completely.

WATERSPOUT

A patio or a quiet corner of the garden can be magically enhanced by the addition of a waterspout. A gentle stream of water spouts through a mask, set into a brick wall topped by an arch, and splashes onto a couple of splash tiles protruding from the wall before tumbling into a reservoir pool. If you enjoy the therapeutic sight and sound of falling water, this striking project will make an exciting feature.

🕐 **TIME**

Five days (add a day if you need to build a foundation).

Special Tips

Do not leave small children unattended if there is a water feature in the garden.

YOU WILL NEED

For a wall, waterspout and reservoir 4' 10" (1.47m) high, 37" (94.8cm) wide and 31½" (80.5cm) deep

 Materials

- Bricks: 205
- Tiles: 24 tiles, 9 ½" (24.5cm) long, 6" (15.2cm) wide and 10mm (⅜") thick
- Mortar: 1 part (55 lbs., or 25kg) cement and 4 parts (220 lbs., or 100kg) sand
- Render: 1 part (55 lbs., or 25kg) cement and 4 parts (220 lbs., or 100kg) coarse sand
- Wood for sticks for center of former: 10 pieces, 7½" (19.3cm) long, 2" (35mm) wide and 1" (22mm) thick
- Wood for trammel: 1 piece, 17½" (44.6cm) long, 2" (35mm) wide and 1" (22mm) thick

- Plywood for former: 2 pieces, 27¼" (69cm) long, 13½" (34.5cm) wide and ¼" (6mm) thick
- Nails: 20 x 1½" (40mm)
- Armored plastic pipe: 13' (4m) x 2" (50mm) in diameter (to protect electric cable and water delivery pipe)
- Flexible plastic pipe (water delivery pipe): 6' 6" (2m) to fit on pump and run through armored pipe 2" (50mm) in diameter)
- Small submersible pump
- Mask: 8½"–11½" (21.5–29cm) high
- Waterproofing paint: 1 quart (1 liter)

 Tools

- Tape measure, straightedge and piece of chalk
- Hacksaw to cut pipe
- Wheelbarrow and bucket
- Shovel and mixing board, or cement mixer
- Claw hammer

- Bricklayer's trowel and pointing trowel
- Bricklayer's hammer and club hammer
- Brick chisel
- Level
- General-purpose saw
- Jigsaw

WATER SETS THE MOOD

Fountains, waterfalls, cascades and waterspouts all make great garden or patio features—the sight and sound of water trickling or splashing into a pool below is mesmerizing and relaxing. The waterspout is a fairly traditional feature in formal, classical gardens, but is also perfect for modern gardens of all descriptions.

This design has the advantage of being freestanding, but most waterspout designs rely on fixing a mask to an existing wall, which entails installing pipework within the wall for the water and power supplies, and this is quite an engineering job. With this project, you don't need an existing wall (but you can build it in front of a wall) and the pipework is concealed within a cavity at the back of the structure.

You may like to consider variations in the overall shape of the structure (perhaps smaller, or squared off at the top), or add decoration such as ornate tile details. You may prefer a different type of wall mask: we have chosen a strong character, but you could have something more restrained like a lion's head, or even design and make something of your own in clay or copper.

Cross-Section View of the Waterspout

Front View Showing the Former During Construction

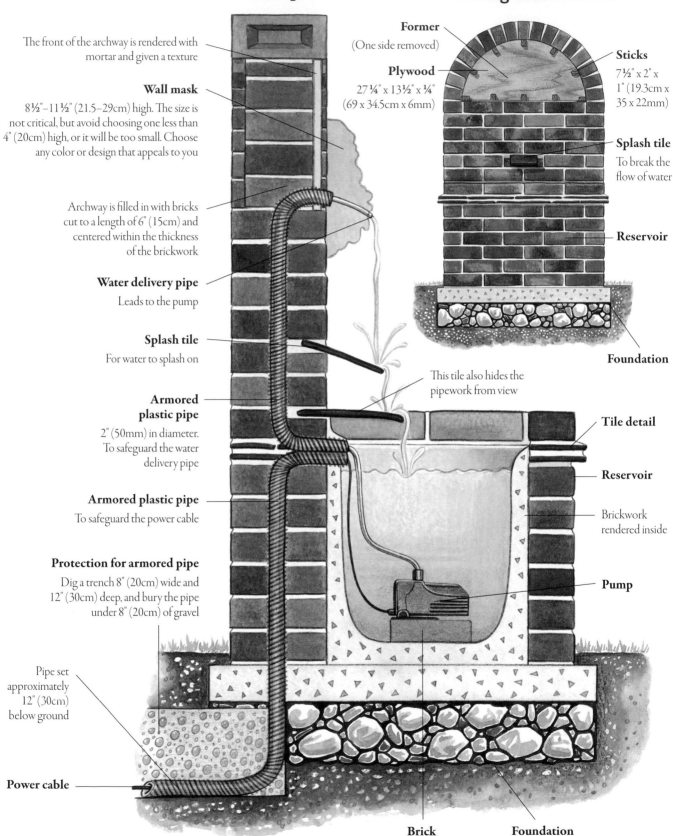

The front of the archway is rendered with mortar and given a texture

Wall mask

8½"–11½" (21.5–29cm) high. The size is not critical, but avoid choosing one less than 4" (20cm) high, or it will be too small. Choose any color or design that appeals to you

Archway is filled in with bricks cut to a length of 6" (15cm) and centered within the thickness of the brickwork

Water delivery pipe

Leads to the pump

Splash tile

For water to splash on

Armored plastic pipe

2" (50mm) in diameter. To safeguard the water delivery pipe

Armored plastic pipe

To safeguard the power cable

Protection for armored pipe

Dig a trench 8" (20cm) wide and 12" (30cm) deep, and bury the pipe under 8" (20cm) of gravel

Pipe set approximately 12" (30cm) below ground

Power cable

Former
(One side removed)

Plywood
27 ¼" x 13½" x ¼"
(69 x 34.5cm x 6mm)

Sticks
7½" x 2" x 1" (19.3cm x 35 x 22mm)

Splash tile
To break the flow of water

Reservoir

Foundation

This tile also hides the pipework from view

Tile detail

Reservoir

Brickwork rendered inside

Pump

Brick   **Foundation**

Exploded View of the Waterspout

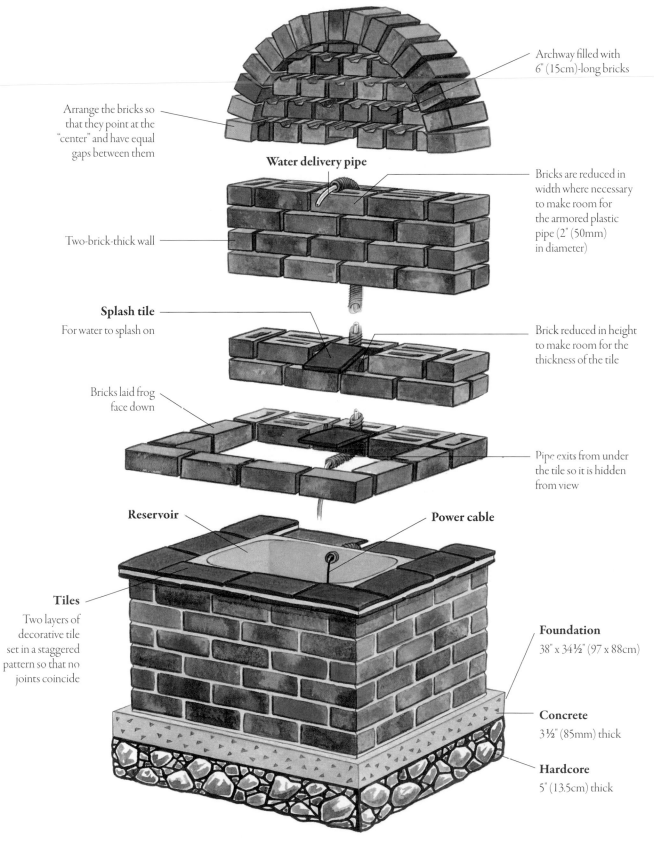

Archway filled with 6" (15cm)-long bricks

Arrange the bricks so that they point at the "center" and have equal gaps between them

Water delivery pipe

Bricks are reduced in width where necessary to make room for the armored plastic pipe (2" (50mm) in diameter)

Two-brick-thick wall

Splash tile
For water to splash on

Brick reduced in height to make room for the thickness of the tile

Bricks laid frog face down

Pipe exits from under the tile so it is hidden from view

Reservoir

Power cable

Tiles
Two layers of decorative tile set in a staggered pattern so that no joints coincide

Foundation
38" x 34½" (97 x 88cm)

Concrete
3½" (85mm) thick

Hardcore
5" (13.5cm) thick

Back wall

Incorporate a second wall at the back of the box

Bond

Build the wall using a running bond

Pipes

Build in two armored pipes—one for water and one for power

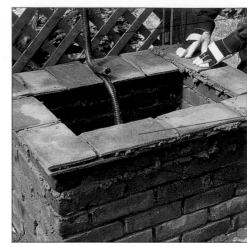

Coping tiles

Top the wall with a double-tile coping

Courses

After every few courses, scrape off excess mortar and clean up the joints between the bricks

1 Find a firm area of patio to build on (with a suitable foundation—see page 35), or construct a level foundation using 5" (13.5cm) of compacted hardcore and 3½" (85mm) of concrete. Mark out the area of the brickwork. Build the reservoir: a simple box shape that incorporates a second wall at the back for housing the pipes. Cut bricks to fit around the armored pipe containing the electric cable.

2 Continue building until you have completed six courses. Lay two courses of tile on ⅜" (10mm)-thick mortar. Overlap the joints as shown, and avoid cutting them if possible. If the tiles are curved, lay them so the bottom layer curves upward and the top layer curves downward. Position the armored pipe for the water delivery pipe.

Splash tile

The distance the tiles protrude, and their angle, affect the way the water falls. Experiment with tiles propped up in position under the mask before starting construction. Pour water through the mask to ascertain how the tiles should be placed for best effect. Take measurements from this mock-up

3 To top the reservoir, lay a line of bricks (frog face down) around the box shape. Finish the joint between the bricks and the tiles with an angled mortar detail. Fix a splash tile into the back wall. Continue building the back wall, cutting bricks where necessary to fit around the water delivery pipe. Refer to the drawings to see how the bricks are laid for best effect.

Helpful Hint

Some of the bricks around the pipe require cutting lengthwise, but for the rest it is enough just to break off the corner with a hammer.

Trammel
Use the trammel to draw semicircles with a radius of 13½" (34.5cm)

Former
Plywood or other scrap wood

Arch
Run bricks around the arch, laying them on their stretcher face

Arch bricks
Use a bit of scrap tile to space the arch bricks

Former
Prop up the former on wedges of wood

4 Complete building the back wall, incorporating a second splash tile and finishing with the water delivery pipe sticking out of the center of the cavity. Make a wooden former for the arch shape: mark semicircles with a 13½" (34.5cm) radius on the plywood using a trammel (see page 46). Cut out with the jigsaw. Join the pieces together as described in the Tudor Arch Wall Niche project on pages 124–129.

5 Place the former on small scraps of wood and practice placing bricks (on their stretcher face) around the curve. When you are confident and ready to start, lay each brick on a generous angled bed of mortar, and tap it down into position. If you need to make major corrections, it is better to start again with fresh mortar. Remove the former by pulling out the scraps of wood beneath.

Rendering
Cover the recessed arch with mortar and create a grooved texture with a piece of scrap wood

Pipe
As you render around the pipe, make sure that it doesn't slip back into the wall

6 Brick up the back of the wall under the arch with bricks that have been reduced in length and laid with the header faces (ends) facing forwards. Leave the water delivery pipe poking out at the front, level with the bottom of the arch. Render the arch recess and texture it with a piece of wood. Render the inside of the reservoir pool with mortar made with coarse sand, allow to dry and coat with waterproofing paint. After a few days, fit the mask and install the pump.

GLOSSARY

Backfilling: To fill or pack a cavity (behind a wall or in a foundation trench hole) with earth in order to bring the ground up to the desired level.

Bedding: The process of pressing a brick, slab or stone into a bed or layer of wet mortar and ensuring that it is level.

Buttering: The act of using a trowel during bricklaying to cover some part of a brick with wet mortar, prior to setting it in position on a bed of mortar.

Compacting: Using a sledgehammer or the weight of the body to press down a layer of sand, earth or hardcore.

Coursing: Part of the process of bricklaying–bedding a number of bricks on a bed of mortar in order to build a course (a horizontal layer of bricks).

Curing time: The time taken for mortar or concrete to become firm and stable. "Part-cured" means that the mortar or concrete is firm enough to bear a small amount of weight.

Floating: The procedure of using a metal, plastic or wooden float to skim wet concrete or mortar to a smooth and level finish.

Hardcore: Scrap bricks, stone and concrete crushed with a sledgehammer and leveled to provide drainage and support beneath a foundation. Alternatively, drainage rock, gravel or graded base can be used.

Leveling: Using a level to decide whether or not a structure or brick is level (horizontally parallel to the ground, or vertically at right angles to the ground), and then making adjustments to bring individual bricks into line.

Marking out: Using string, stakes and a tape measure to variously set out the area of a foundation on the ground. Also to mark an individual brick in readiness for cutting.

Pecking: Using the edge of a large trowel or the chisel end of a bricklayer's hammer to nibble the ragged edge of a part-cut brick back to a marked line.

Planning: The procedure of considering a project, viewing the site, making drawings, working out quantities and costs, prior to starting work. Thorough planning is vital in order to avoid hold-ups and the wastage of materials.

Pointing: Using a trowel, stick or a tool of your choice to bring mortar joints to the desired finish.

Raking out: Using a trowel to rake out some part of the mortar from between courses, so that the edges of the bricks are clearly and crisply revealed.

Sighting: To judge by eye whether or not a cut, joint or structure is level or true. To look down or along a wall in order to determine whether or not the structure is level.

Siting: Deciding where on the site—in the garden or on the plot—the structure is going to be placed. The aspect, sun, shade and proximity to the house may need to be taken into consideration.

Sourcing: Questioning suppliers by phone, email or letter, in order to make decisions concerning the best source for materials–especially sand, cement and bricks.

Tamping: The act of using a length of wood to compact and level wet concrete.

Trial run or dry run: Setting out the components of a structure, without using concrete or mortar, in order to ascertain whether or not the pattern of bricks is going to work out.

Trimming: Using a hammer or the edge of a large trowel to cut and sculpt a brick to a good finish.

Watering: Wetting bricks at the start of a work session, prior to bedding them on mortar.

Wire brushing: Using a wire-bristled brush to remove dry mortar from the face of bricks, for example on a wall, or the surface of a path or patio.

INDEX

INDEX